ILFORD TO SHENFIELD

Dave Brennand
Series editor Vic Mitchell

MP Middleton Press

Cover picture: No. 70000 Britannia *speeds towards London on 4th May 1956 and passes Ilford Car Sheds signal box with "The Hook Continental" boat train from Harwich Parkeston Quay. The Britannia class graced the route for several years and gave good performance. (British Rail)*

Published December 2002
First reprint June 2006

ISBN 1 901706 97 4

© *Middleton Press, 2002*

Design   Deborah Esher
Typesetting   Barbara Mitchell

Published by
       Middleton Press
       Easebourne Lane
       Midhurst, West Sussex
       GU29 9AZ
Tel: 01730 813169
Fax: 01730 812601
Email: info@middletonpress.co.uk
www.middletonpress.co.uk

Printed & bound by Biddles Ltd, Kings Lynn

INDEX

86	Brentwood	1	Ilford
80	Brentwood Goods	7	Ilford Carriage Sidings
31	Chadwell Heath	46	Romford
59	Gidea Park	67	Romford Factory
25	Goodmayes	20	Seven Kings
73	Harold Wood	102	Shenfield

ACKNOWLEDGEMENTS

I would like to extend my sincere thanks to the photographers for allowing me to reproduce their work. The following people gave inspiration, guidance and valuable historical background information: - Bob Clow, Jim Connor, Andy Grimmett, Richard Hill, Roger Kingston, John Watling and Gordon Wells. Special thanks go to Alan Young for drawing the excellent route maps. Godfrey Croughton who kindly supplied the ticket copies. A few of the photographs taken by myself have been obtained during the course of my work as a railway employee. My greatest thanks go to my wife Belinda for her typing, proof reading, computing skills and tolerance.

GEOGRAPHICAL SETTING

The Ilford to Shenfield route follows a relatively straight course through the Essex countryside north of the River Thames. Much of the line is built on the Taplow Gravel Terrace and Essex Clay at the eastern flank. From an altitude of a mere 50 feet at Ilford the line is mainly level until Harold Wood, when it then rises steeply at up to 1 in 80 to over 250 feet at Ingrave summit between Brentwood and Shenfield. The line crosses the shallow valleys and narrow streams of Seven Kings Water, Mayes Brook, the Rivers Rom and Ingrebourne.

When opened in the 19th century, the line traversed great tracts of farmland and forest. However, since 1900 the vast majority of the line has been enveloped by creeping urban and commercial development. Open countryside can still be glimpsed however, between Harold Wood and Brentwood, albeit scarred by the unsightly intrusion of the M25 motorway.

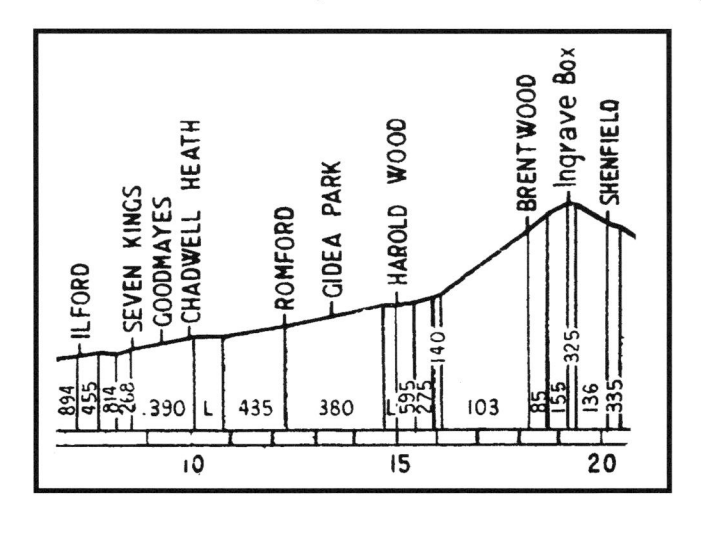

HISTORICAL BACKGROUND

The Eastern Counties Railway had grand ideas back in 1834 to link London with Norwich. Spurred on by the successes of first the Stockton & Darlington, then the Liverpool & Manchester Railways, it believed that East Anglia was crying out for a railway to connect the important towns of that time. However, they did not have whole-hearted support, as many landowners rejected their ideas. Despite the protestations, a Bill was presented to Parliament on 19th February 1836 and Royal Assent was granted the following July. Ilford therefore first appeared on a railway map in 1839 with the opening of the ECR line from London to Romford on 18th June. The engineer John Braithwaite built the line to a gauge of 5 feet. The standard gauge was adopted in 1844. At that time Ilford was surrounded by parkland and the nearby Hainault Forest. The next station was Romford, already an established market town of modest size. The further growth of these places was almost entirely due to the arrival of the railway, which opened up a whole 'new world' to passengers more used to horse-drawn carriages.

Much of the line between Ilford and Chadwell Heath was in a cutting at that time. A consequential need for affordable housing inevitably followed in the railway navvies' wake as London's suburbia expanded into the countryside. The ECR chose a site just east of Romford for its locomotive works - although sited in what we now call Gidea Park - the Romford Factory produced, albeit briefly, some of the earliest locomotives for East Anglia's railways until 1847 when Stratford Works took on the role. The station at Brentwood opened on 1st July 1840, then became a temporary terminus due to problems with finance and construction. A locomotive turntable was installed at Brentwood in the early 1840s owing to this being 'the end of the line' until the official opening to Colchester on 29th March 1843. There was a need from the onset of train working for banking engines at Brentwood, due to the steep climb beyond.

Interestingly, and an indication of how very undeveloped Shenfield was in 1843 (the year of opening), the station suffered from a severe lack of patronage and closed in 1850. It was given a new lease of life in 1887 as Shenfield & Hutton Junction serving the new line to Southend Victoria, which opened in stages until 1889. The formation and growth of the ECR is adequately described in the precursor to this volume, *Liverpool Street to Ilford*. The line between Ilford and Shenfield was just double track with intermediate stations at Romford and Brentwood only. It was very rural, and the ECR did not consider it viable to construct additional stations. The ECR gained a reputation for unreliability and very small returns for its shareholders during the relatively short time that it existed. It must therefore have come as a great relief to all concerned when the Great Eastern Railway was formed in 1862.

The new company, being mindful of the improvements needed, opened Chadwell Heath in 1864 and Harold Wood in 1868. The greatest expansion of housing in the Ilford area took place in the late 1890s, and the GER (seeing huge potential) wasted very little time by quadrupling the tracks from Ilford to a new station at Seven Kings in 1899. The line from here to a junction just short of Romford was quadrupled in 1901 in anticipation of the growth in commuter and freight traffic, and a new station at Goodmayes opened in the same year. The area either side of the line between Goodmayes and Chadwell Heath was occupied by a new marshalling yard, which had opened in 1899. The yard was enlarged in 1910 to keep up with the demands of a growing freight network. The triangular junction between Ilford and Seven Kings, which served Newbury Park and the Hainault loop line, opened in 1903.

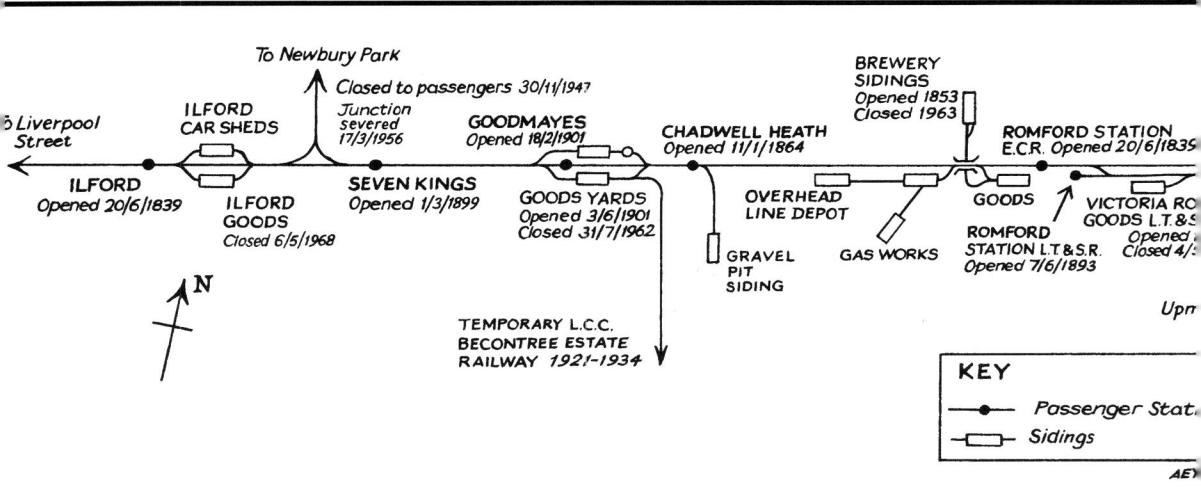

A burgeoning estate for the wealthier classes in the area east of Romford gave rise to a new GER station called Squirrels Heath & Gidea Park in 1910. Arch rivals, the London Tilbury & Southend Railway had opened Emerson Park & Great Nemes on their nearby Upminster - Romford line in the previous year, and the GER saw this as a threat to their income.

In the 1923 grouping the Shenfield line came under the control of the newly formed London & North Eastern Railway who looked upon the ex-GER lines as a poor relation to the more prestigious ex-Great Northern lines from Kings Cross when it came to express services, motive power and rolling stock. The LNER came under growing criticism in the late 1920s for the chronic overcrowding on the Liverpool Street - Shenfield section, as all the suburban and main line traffic fought for space beyond Romford where the lines reduced from four to two tracks. The LNER - with the aid of a Government grant - announced in 1931 that they were to embark on a huge engineering feat to alleviate the bottleneck, by widening the Gidea Park - Shenfield section to four tracks and installing colour light signalling.

Work had already started the previous year to widen the Romford - Gidea Park section. Huge amounts of earth were moved from the new widened cuttings and transported using a small temporary narrow gauge contractor's railway alongside the mainline to form a new embankment between Harold Wood and Brentwood. Beyond Brentwood reinforced concrete retaining walls still hold back the Essex countryside on the steep 1 in 85 climb to Shenfield, as the line passes under the imposing Seven Arches Bridge. The stations at Harold Wood, Brentwood and Shenfield were extensively rebuilt at the same time, giving long-suffering passengers better facilities and train services. East of Shenfield, in order to alleviate conflicting movements, a dive-under was constructed for the benefit of Southend trains.

Despite all this effort, passenger numbers continued to rise, which prompted the grandiose LNER and London Transport New Works Programme of 1935 for electrification at 1500 volts DC, of the Liverpool Street to Shenfield section, a plan which was rudely interrupted by the outbreak of hostilities in 1939. The LNER publicly forecast that this work would be completed by the end of 1940 at a cost of £3,500,000, but the cruel turn of events delayed this construction by another seven years. The plan also stated that the triangular junction at Seven Kings was to be severed when LT took over running of services on the Hainault loop with a new underground connection between Stratford and Leyton. Again, due to the interruption of the Second World War this was not fully opened until 1947. The triangular junction at Seven Kings was therefore very short lived, and the Eastern curve was not used by regular passenger trains, only freight, empty stock workings and excursions. Many old signal boxes were swept away at this time and the cumbersome manual lever frames replaced by modern electric interlocking as fewer boxes were required. By the time that the electrification and resignalling were finished there had been a huge upheaval in the management of the railways in general.

The formation of British Railways on 1st January 1948 heralded a new era and the introduction of the new electric service was finally delivered in September 1949. Class 306 electric units took over all the inner suburban traffic - a task which they performed admirably for over 40 years. To maintain these new units, Ilford Car Sheds was opened in 1949 on the site of the old Ilford Carriage Sidings.

Since Privatisation in 1996 all the suburban traffic and the Clacton, Harwich and Braintree services have been operated by First Group plc. Anglia Railways operate some Ipswich and all Norwich services. This arrangement will change in 2004 when all services to and from Liverpool Street including WAGN services will become the responsibility of one operator after refranchising.

I. Route diagram. (A.Young)

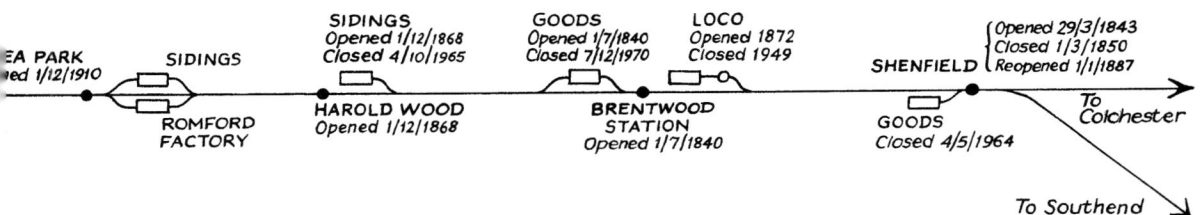

PASSENGER SERVICES

The first trains in 1839 only operated from Mile End to Romford, and to use the word 'frequent' would not adequately describe the service. Even when Shoreditch and Brentwood opened the following year there were only eight trains per day. The last of these reached its destination around 8pm, so no late night revellers back then! During ECR ownership services on the Ilford to Shenfield section were rather sparse. With only two intermediate stations at Romford and Brentwood, there was little justification for a suburban service and main line trains provided all services. Only a dozen passenger trains per day operated each way in the late 1850s. Not until GER days was there any real improvement. With the opening of Liverpool Street in 1874 services could at last be increased, and such was the growth in the following decades that some trains to Ilford, Woodford (via Newbury Park) and Brentwood used Fenchurch Street instead.

The table below indicates the growth pattern and shows the number of down trains calling at Romford in selected years.

	Weekdays	Sundays
1850	8	5
1869	14	6
1885	27	15
1899	48	22

With additional passengers coming into London from the new Southend line that opened in 1889, the pressure was really on the GER to find innovative ways of coping with the demand. Truly intensive services over the Ilford to Romford section started in the late 1890s, when house building in the Ilford district was at its zenith. It is no exaggeration to say that services had to be doubled to cope with the demand between 1897 and 1900. As the urbanisation spread eastwards, so the GER had to provide more and more trains in the wake of the house builders. Services gradually improved until the outbreak of World War I in 1914, which for the next four years caused severe disruption at times. The inter-war years would not have been easy for the intrepid passengers, as overcrowding and engineering works became a way of life. Improvements to services finally came in the mid-1930s after the widening. The greatest step forward finally came with the introduction of the new electric service in 1949. Some peak trains terminated at Chadwell Heath or Brentwood. The pattern of frequency however remained largely unchanged for several decades.

The introduction of new class 315 electric units in 1978 caused the demise of the familiar class 306s. Then class 321s were introduced in 1988 finally ousting most of the life-expired 1950s slam-door stock. First Great Eastern took over train operation in 1996 and in 2000 implemented the most frequent services ever offered between London and Shenfield under the name Metro. This service coincided with the speeding up of Liverpool Street - Southend Victoria line trains which no longer called at Gidea Park, Harold Wood and Brentwood, resulting in increased journey times to and from these stations.

February 1850

ILFORD

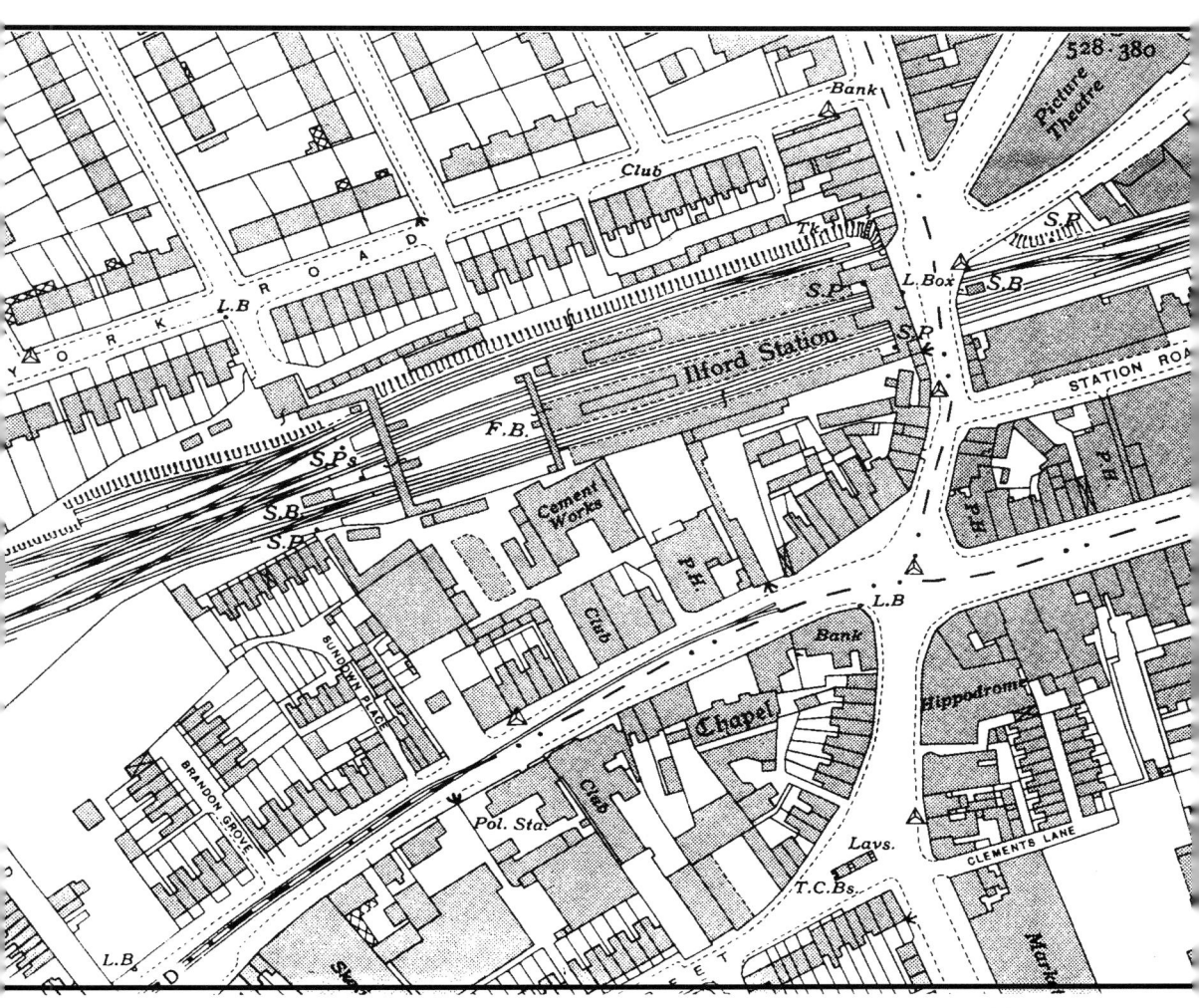

II. The 1839 station had only two platforms, and the widening which was completed in 1897 included a bay platform. This OS map of 1938 shows the track formation just before work commenced on the Ilford Flyover in that year. Note that Ilford East Junction signal box is shown.

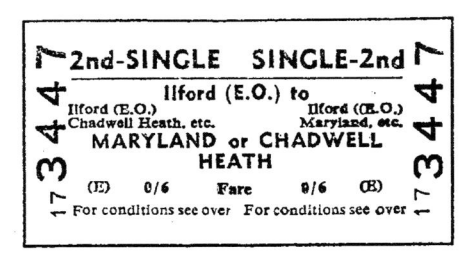

1. We start our journey with a delightful overall view of the London end of the station looking east. The single-storey building on the left is the York Road ticket office. The engine in the centre of this view would have just run-round its train, as many local services terminated at Ilford after arriving from Fenchurch Street or Liverpool Street. The date is 1910 and the station is a hive of activity. (British Rail)

2. In this view we are looking south from the north side of the line. There is a gated entrance to a short siding owned by local coal merchants. The bridge in the foreground carries the railway over Mill Road, which gained its name from the former Ilford Paper Mill Company's complex that dominates the background. A British Telecom building subsequently overshadowed the scene. (British Rail)

3. We now stand with our back to the station looking west towards London. This view was taken from the footbridge. Class D16 'Claud' 4-4-0 no. 8782 approaches with a Liverpool Street - Southend service on 11th June 1938 comprising a rather motley collection of coaches. Work on the familiar landmark of Ilford flyover started later in the same year. (H.C.Casserley)

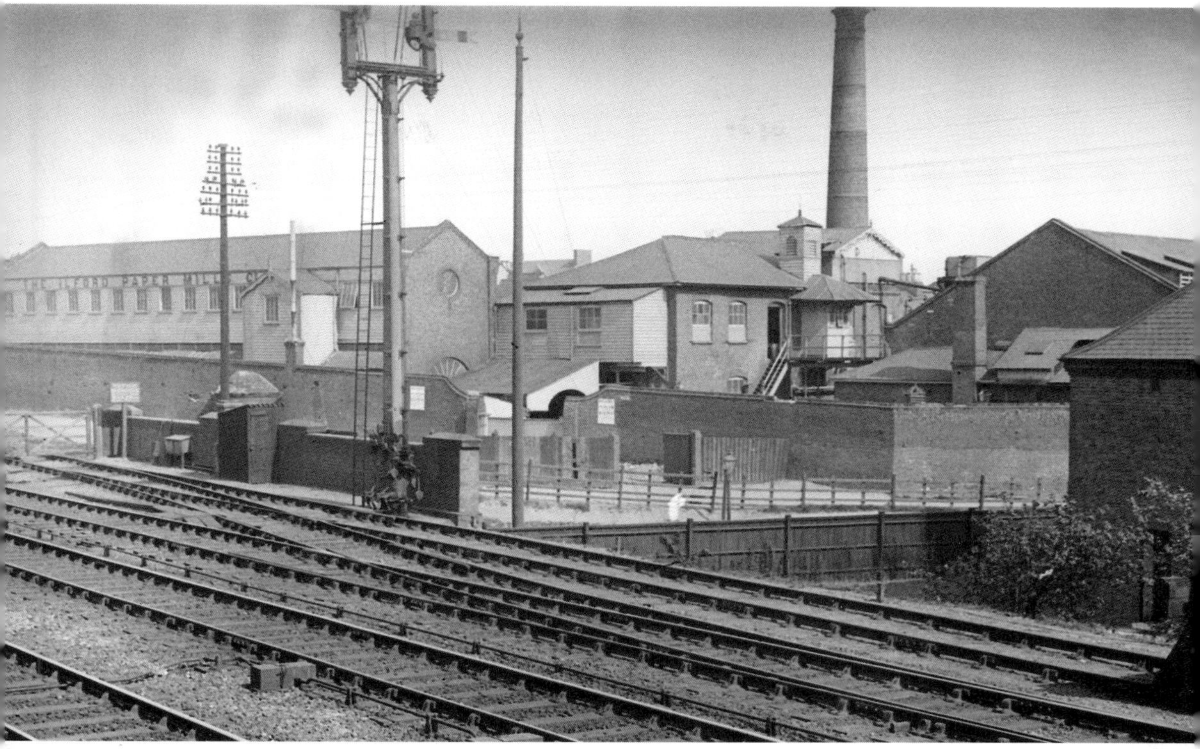

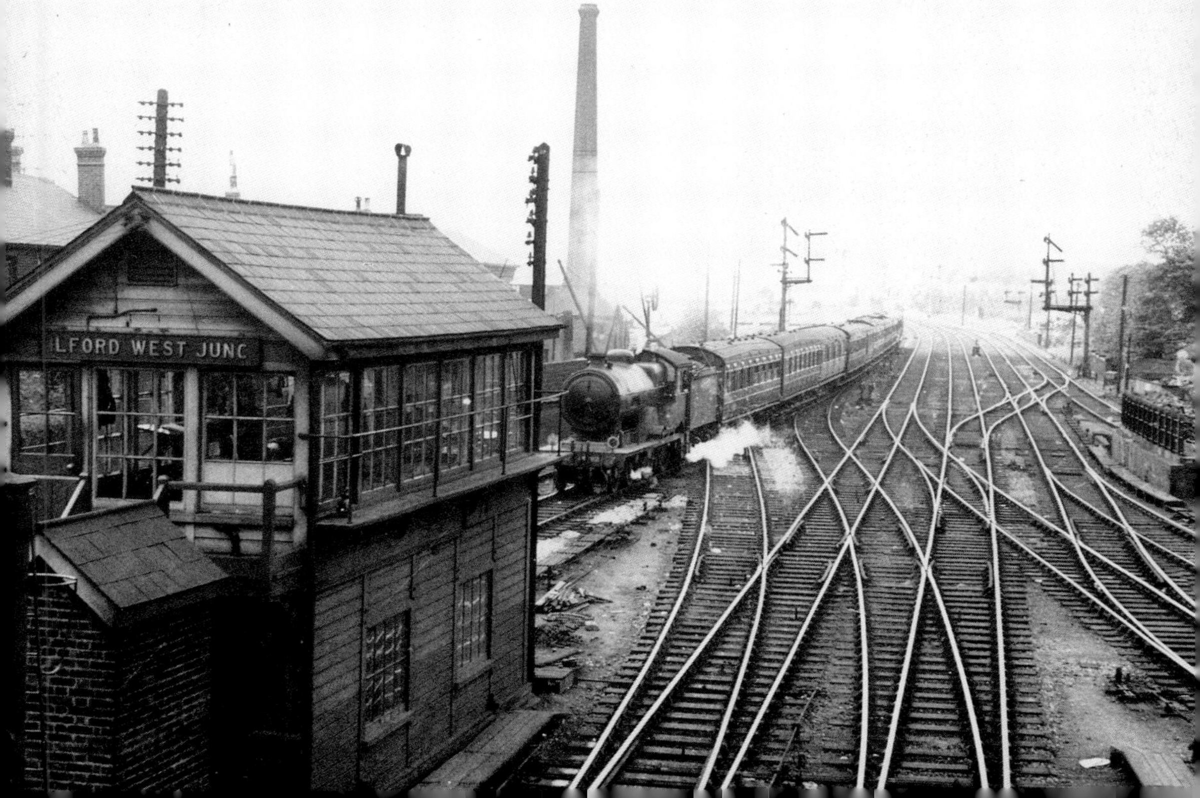
LFORD WEST JUNC

4.   The signalman in the busy Ilford West Junction signal box enters the passing Liverpool Street - Gidea Park service hauled by class F4 2-4-2 no. 7178 into his train register. Again, we look west from the footbridge on 11th June 1938. Electrification caused the demise of this box and it closed on 14th August 1949. (H.C.Casserley)

5.   We now look east and see the parcel footbridge. The main lines are on our right, whilst the slow lines are on our left in this 1937 view. This arrangement caused a huge number of conflicting movements approaching Liverpool Street, as suburban and main line trains swapped tracks to enter their respective platforms. This was the reason for the building of Ilford flyover. (H.C.Casserley)

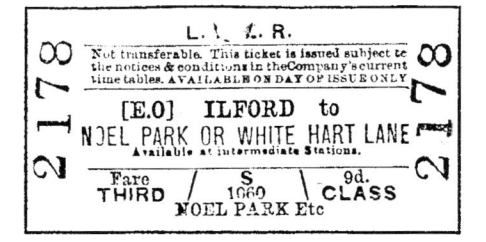

6.   Class 15 Bo-Bo no. D8204 disturbs the peace on an otherwise quiet Sunday, as it passes through Ilford with an overhead wiring train in 1970. (Authors collection)

ILFORD

BEST ALWAYS
REYNOLDS Ford SERVICE

PYRUMA WORKS

ILFORD

THE FIR

D8204

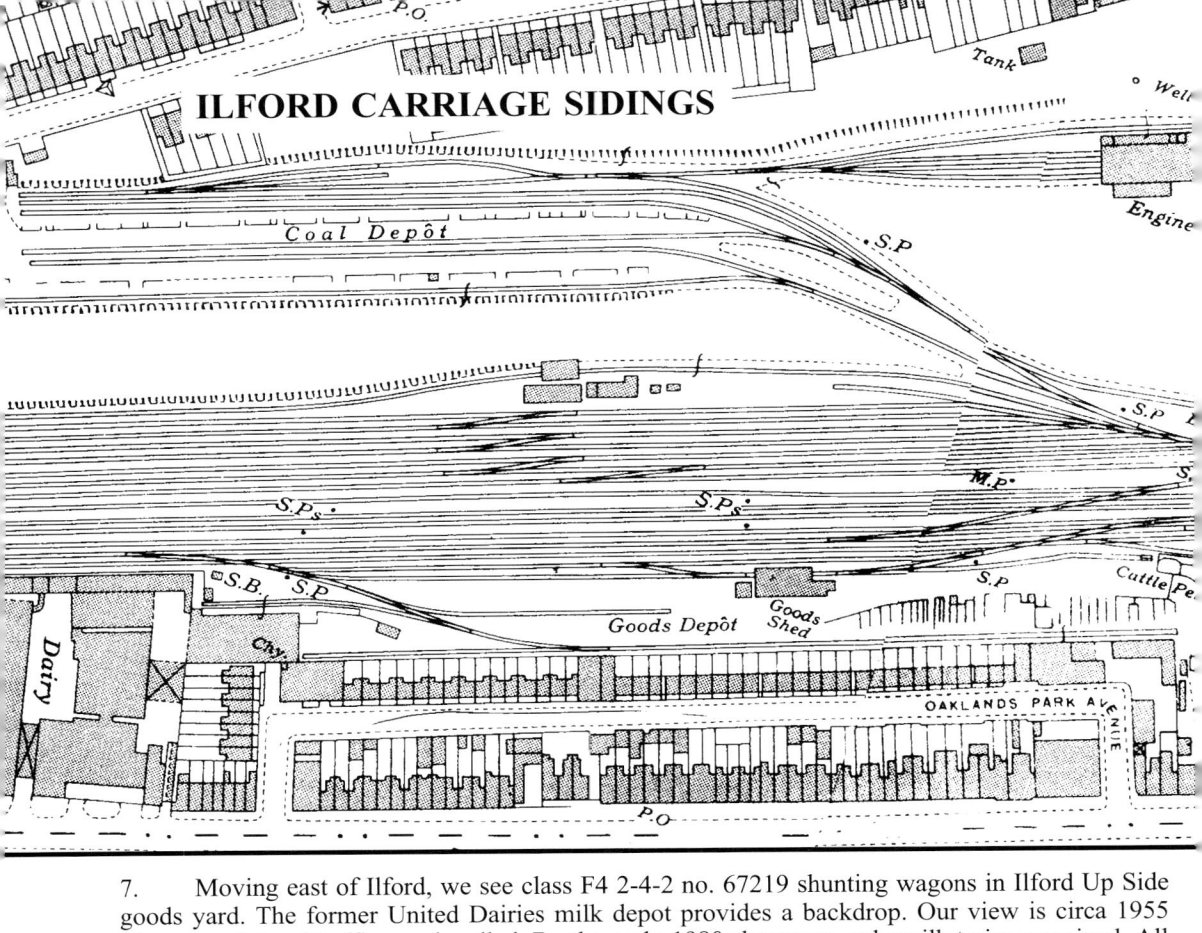

ILFORD CARRIAGE SIDINGS

7. Moving east of Ilford, we see class F4 2-4-2 no. 67219 shunting wagons in Ilford Up Side goods yard. The former United Dairies milk depot provides a backdrop. Our view is circa 1955 when a variety of traffic was handled. By the early 1980s however, only milk trains remained. All traces have since disappeared. (Unknown)

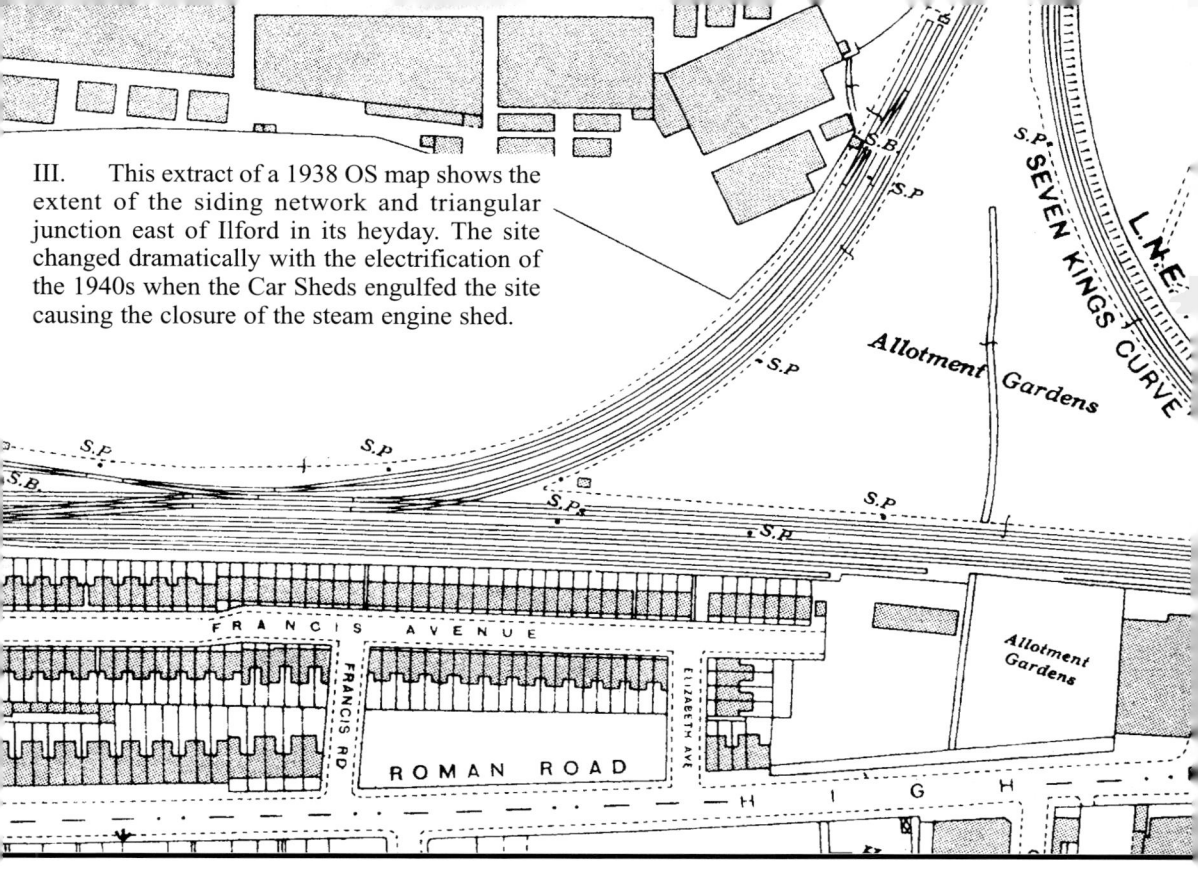

III. This extract of a 1938 OS map shows the extent of the siding network and triangular junction east of Ilford in its heyday. The site changed dramatically with the electrification of the 1940s when the Car Sheds engulfed the site causing the closure of the steam engine shed.

8. Here we are looking at the entrance to Ilford Goods Depot located in Romford Road, which had suffered bomb damage at the height of World War II. This view was taken after repairs had taken place in April 1943, but the sewing machine shop next door is looking rather precarious! The goods office survives, the yard having closed on 6th May 1968. (British Rail)

9. Standing in the Ilford Carriage Sidings signal box looking west during GER days in 1910, we see the goods yard on the south side of the line. A cattle dock is on the left, whilst hidden behind the footbridge support is the goods shed. On the opposite side of the line are rakes of 6-wheeled coaches in the carriage sidings. (British Rail)

10. Again in 1910 we are treated to a view of the extensive nature of the sidings at Ilford, which could accommodate up to 100 short wheelbase coaches. To the far right, a locomotive is coming off the 3-road loco shed. (British Rail)

11. Just 26 years have passed; the scene in 1936 has changed dramatically. Many trains now terminate at Gidea Park, which has caused a noticeable decline in the use of Ilford sidings. The steam shed (just out of view on the far right) has just three years left until closure. Engines were turned on the Newbury Park triangle. (British Rail)

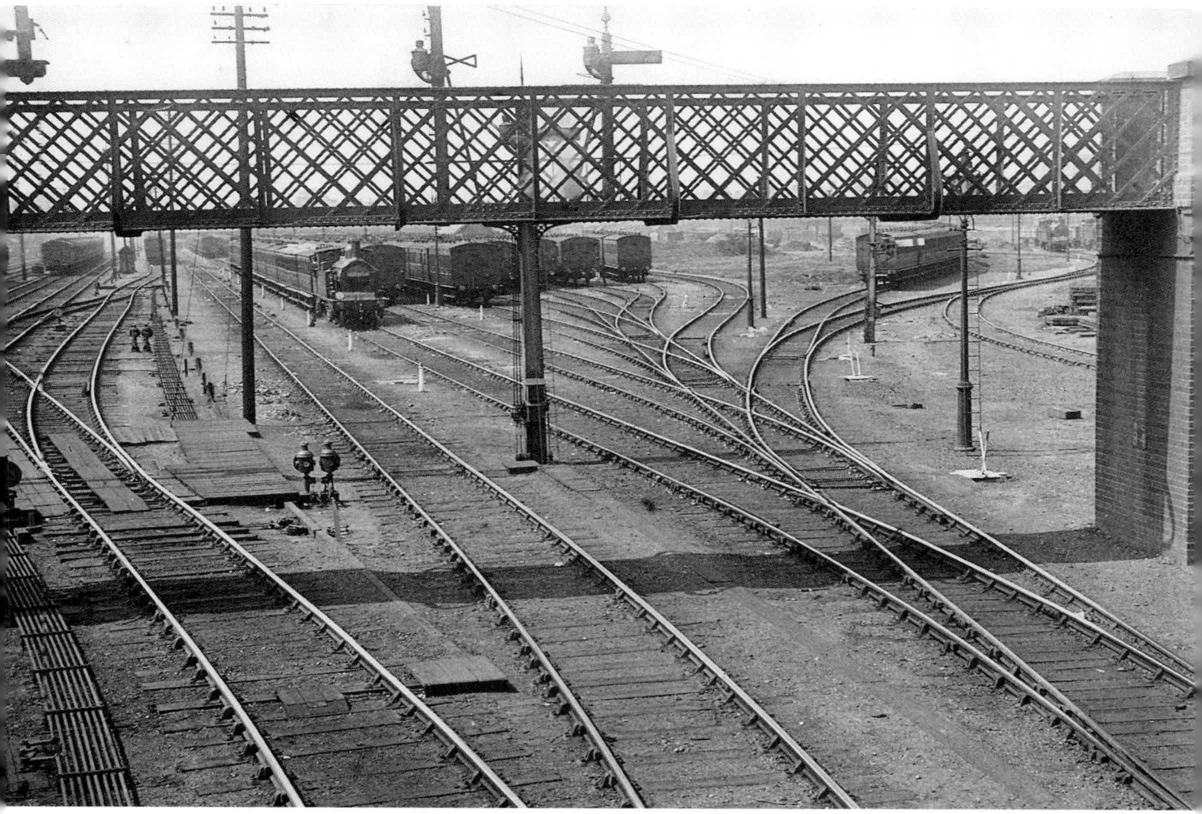

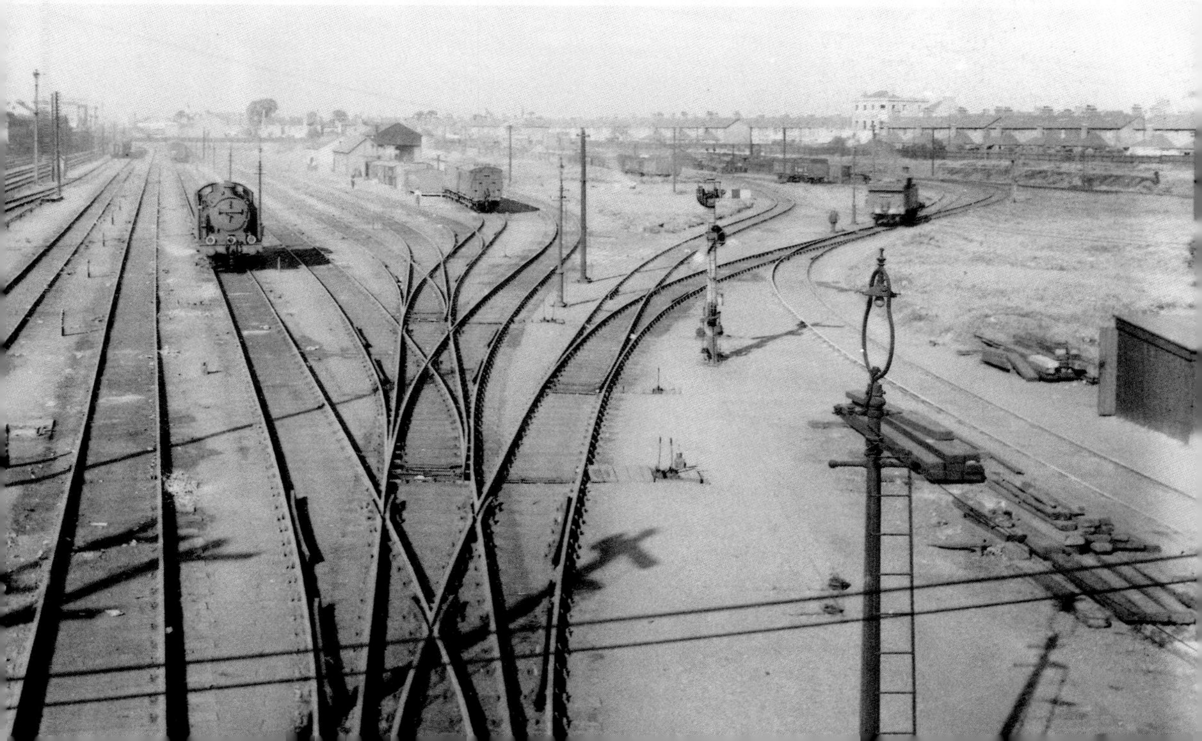

12. We now look east towards Seven Kings station from our vantage-point in Ilford sidings in 1910. In the middle distance we see the branch to Newbury Park curving to the left. (British Rail)

13. Another quarter of a decade later, and the branch to Newbury Park just clings to life in 1936. The wasteland is former allotments. Ilford Carriage Sidings signal box closed on 19th December 1943 and the scene has since been dominated by Ilford's 'New Shed', which opened in 1959. (British Rail)

14. We have moved forward to March 1949 and the first of the 1500 DC electric units has arrived at Ilford Car Sheds. These were widely considered to be 'state of the art' and a far cry from the steam trains they replaced. (British Rail)

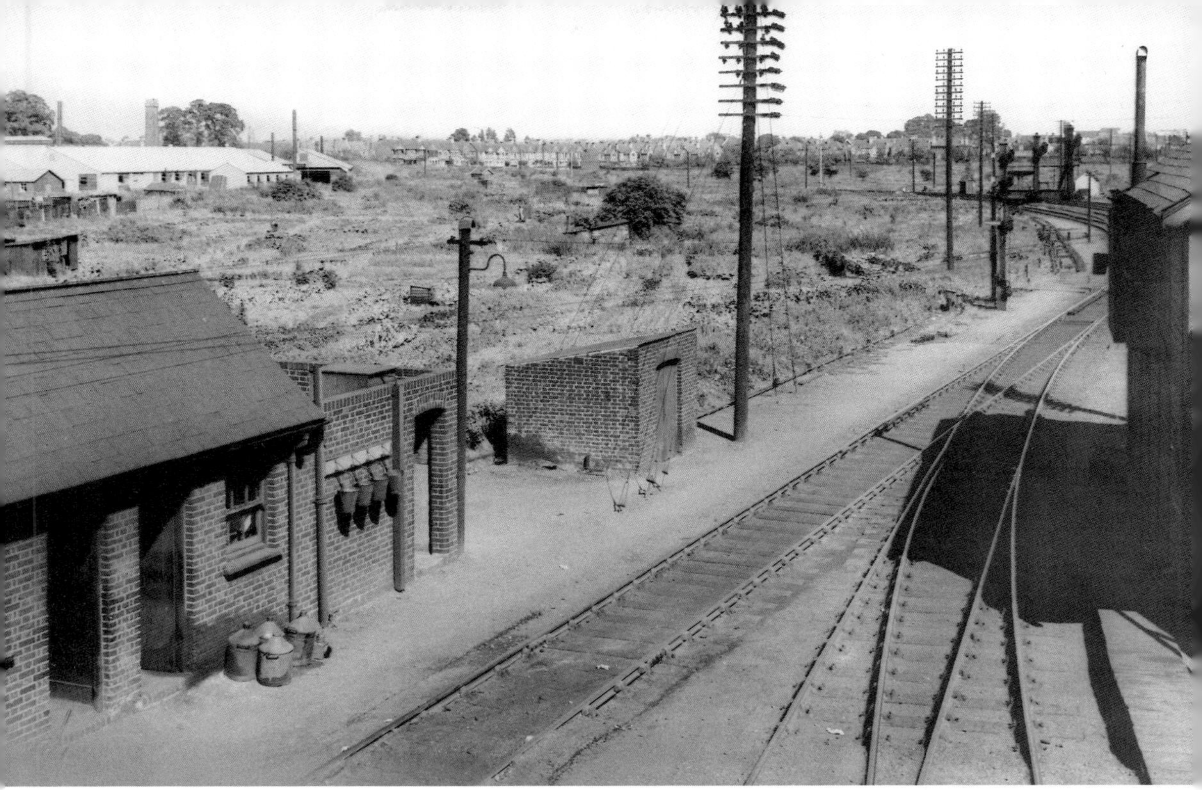

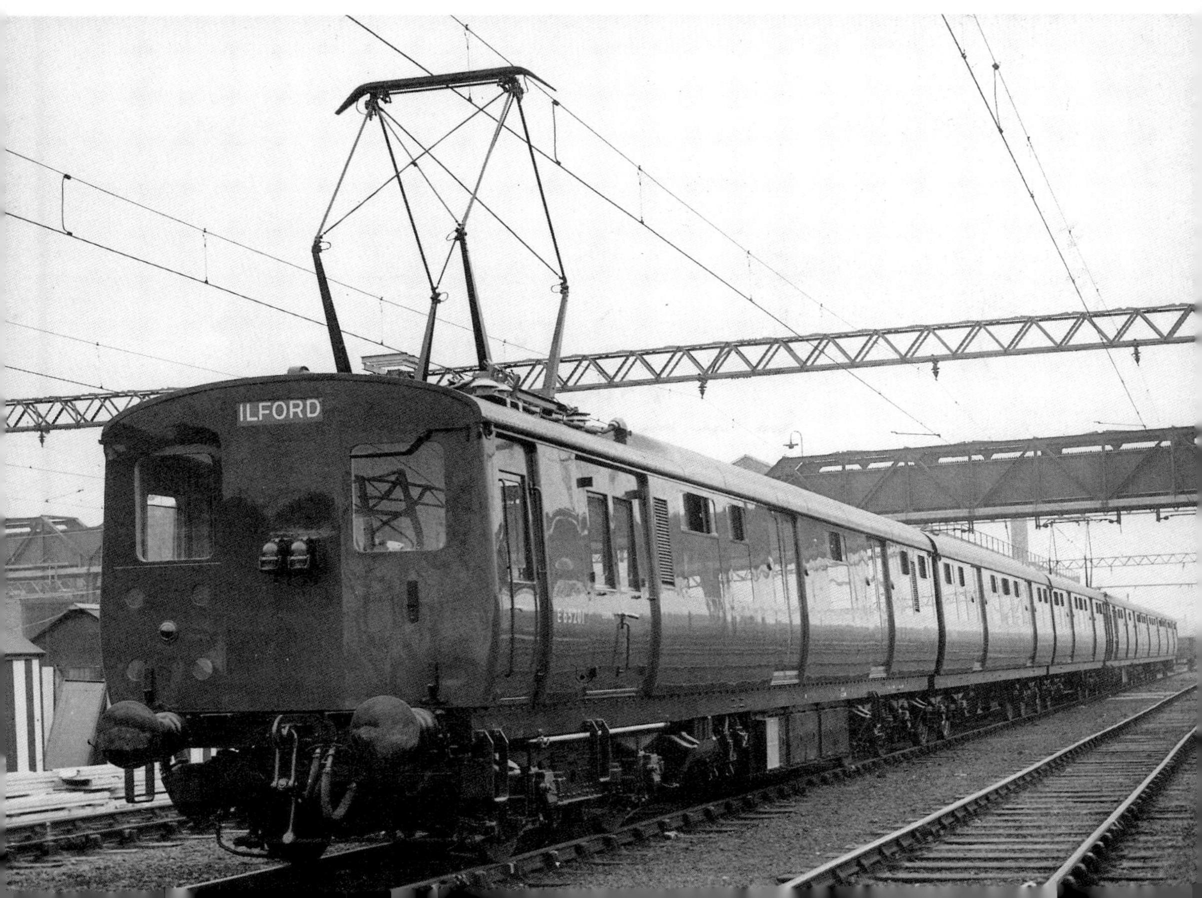
ILFORD

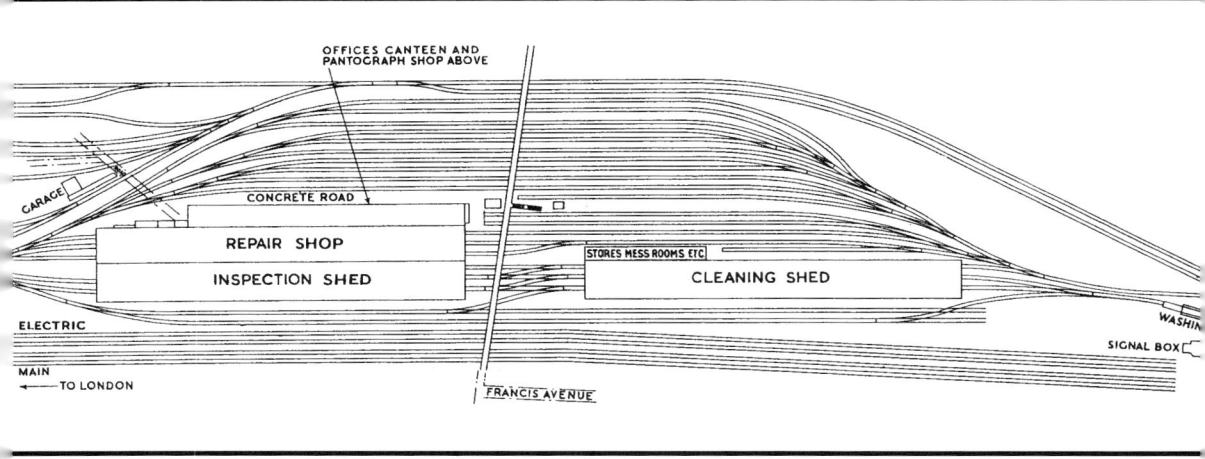

IV.   Car Sheds Diagram.

15.   A most remarkable new lease of life was given to the former North Eastern Railway Bo-Bo electric loco no. 26510 in 1949 as it took on the role of Ilford Depot pilot. It is pictured in the depots' Ley Street sidings. (K. Nunn /LCGB)

16. We now see the Ilford depot pilot on 16th May 1956 engaged in shunting new Southend stock. The loco was affectionately known by drivers as 'Dennis'. In its original form the depot comprised of two large workshops, incorporating an overhead crane, pantograph shop, carriage washing plant and a large canteen. The site was expanded during 1958-59 to accommodate additional units when the 'New Shed' opened at the country end of the yard on the site formerly occupied by the Newbury Park triangle. (T.Wright)

17. The Manchester - Sheffield 1500 DC system had not been completed in time for the testing of the new EM1 Bo-Bo locos. Seen here is no. 26008 at Ilford Car Sheds in 1950. Several of the class members ran trials over former GER metals. (Authors collection)

18. Here we see the country end of Ilford Car Sheds in October 1949. On the left is the inspection shed, whilst the building on the right contains an overhead crane to facilitate body lifting for access to the traction motors within the bogies. (British Rail)

19. Out of 92 units ordered in 1938, there remains one survivor. no. 017 is still used on enthusiasts' weekends and seen here at Ilford depot in October 2001. (D.Brennand)

SEVEN KINGS

20. Looking west from the station, we see Seven Kings West Junction signal box controlling the junction to Newbury Park in 1936. The right-hand arms on the gantry took drivers onto the branch. The box closed on 7th August 1949 when Ilford Car Sheds signal box was commissioned. (R.R. Clow/Harwich Shipping & Railway Museum)

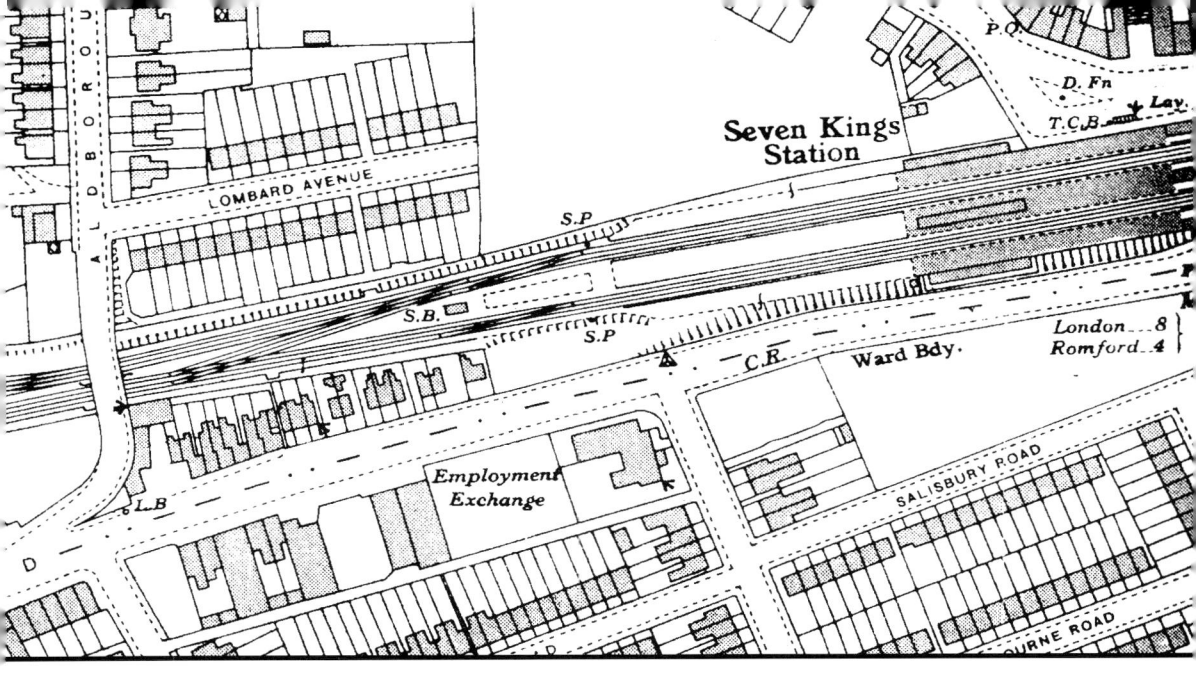

V.　　In order to avoid repeating the earlier mistakes west of Ilford, by providing only suburban line platforms, the GER opted for four platforms at Seven Kings when it opened in 1899, as shown in this 1938 OS extract. The junction from Newbury Park that opened in 1903 is shown joining the slow lines from the left.

21.　　We now stand on the slow line platform looking east in 1930. The LNER 'mint imperial' lamp standards, carry the station name on brown and cream 'lamp tablets'. Passengers await the next Liverpool Street bound service. (D.Brennand coll.)

22. This view of the station entrance dates from 1966 and by good fortune, the building has remained largely unaltered. (J.E.Connor)

23. Standing in the same spot as the 1930 view, we see class 306 unit no. 076 in early BR dark blue, as it departs with a Gidea Park bound service in 1968. The guard exchanges a few words with a member of staff as they pass. (D.Brennand coll.)

24. We look east again in 1974, prior to the demolition of all the platform buildings, which took place in the early 80s. The station now has shutters surrounding the only remaining waiting room, in an effort to curb pointless vandalism. (A.E.Young)

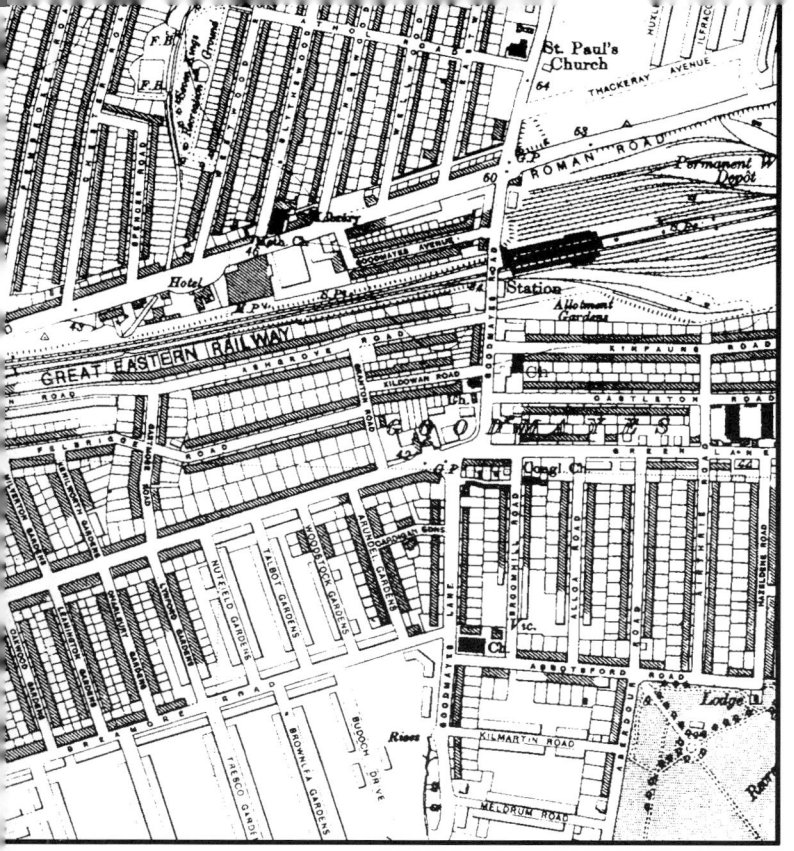

GOODMAYES

VI. This extract from a 1920 OS map shows the extent of the once busy freight yards east of Goodmayes station, which opened in 1901. An engine turntable is provided on the north side of the main lines. The yard had virtually disappeared by 1962.

25. Goodmayes became a target several times during World War II due to being on a strategic route to the eastern ports. Here we see the aftermath of an air raid on 6th April 1940, as we view the devastation looking west. The slow lines remain open, as a class N7 0-6-2 gingerly creeps past the workmen trying to repair the main lines.
(R.R.Clow/Harwich Shipping & Railway Museum)

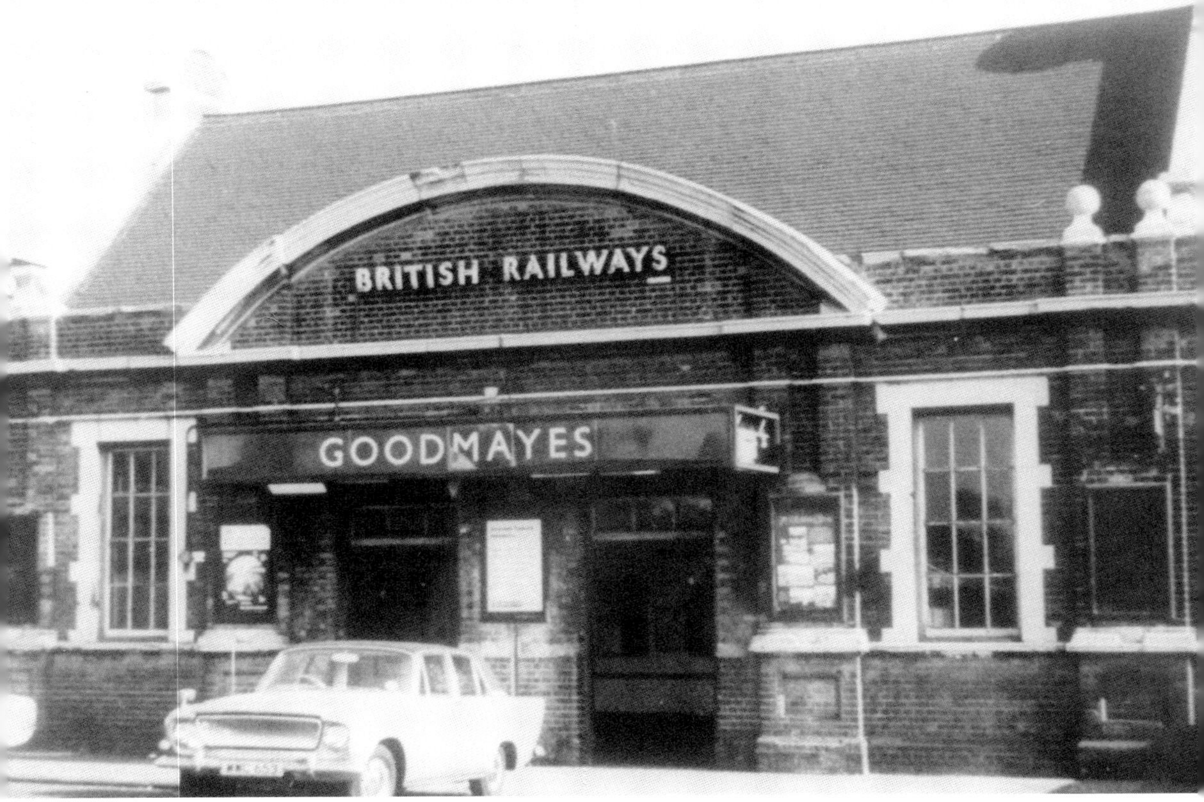
BRITISH RAILWAYS
GOODMAYES

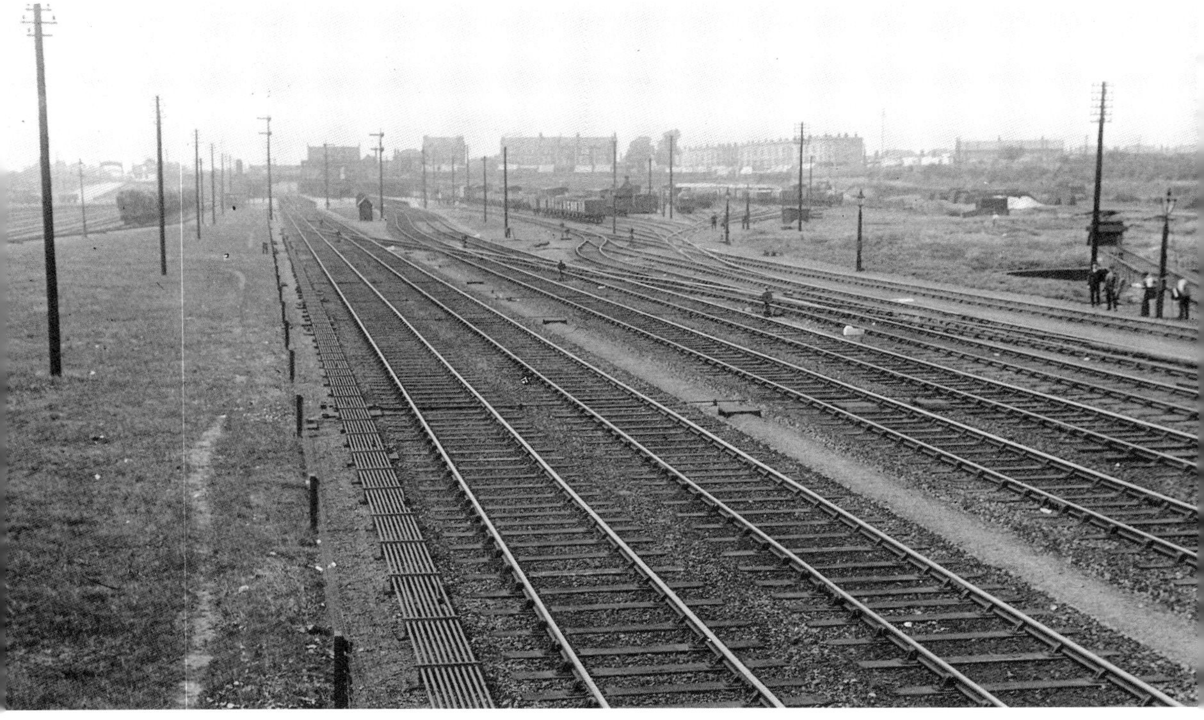

26. The station entrance in Goodmayes Road dates from opening on 8th February 1901. Shown here in 1973, it is an exact copy of the previous station. (J.E.Connor)

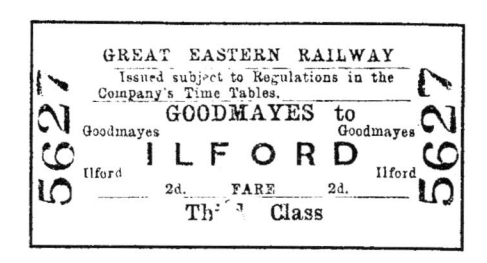

27. Most of the land either side of the line east of Goodmayes was devoted to the goods yards. The foreground shows the locomotive turntable circa 1920. The decline in importance of the yard came about due to the concentration of traffic at Temple Mills, near Stratford in the early 1960s. (British Rail)

28. A tremendous variety of goods wagons are shown here as we look west again in 1936. Some of the wagons still carry pre-grouping company initials! Freight facilities were withdrawn on 31st July 1962. Sadly, the inevitable superstores and car parks gradually occupied the whole vista. (British Rail)

29. Streamlined LNER class B17 4-6-0 no. 2859 *East Anglian* heads a Norwich - Liverpool Street train past Goodmayes East signal box in this evocative view looking east on 28th September 1937. The locomotive carries fully lined apple green livery, whilst Gresley teak coaches follow. (K.Nunn/LCGB)

30. We leave Goodmayes, with a final closer look at Goodmayes East signal box on 2nd September 1936. The box shown here closed in 1949 when a new box opened on the opposite side of the track during the electrification work. This was demolished in 1997 after further resignalling. The area subsequently being controlled from Liverpool Street. (British Rail)

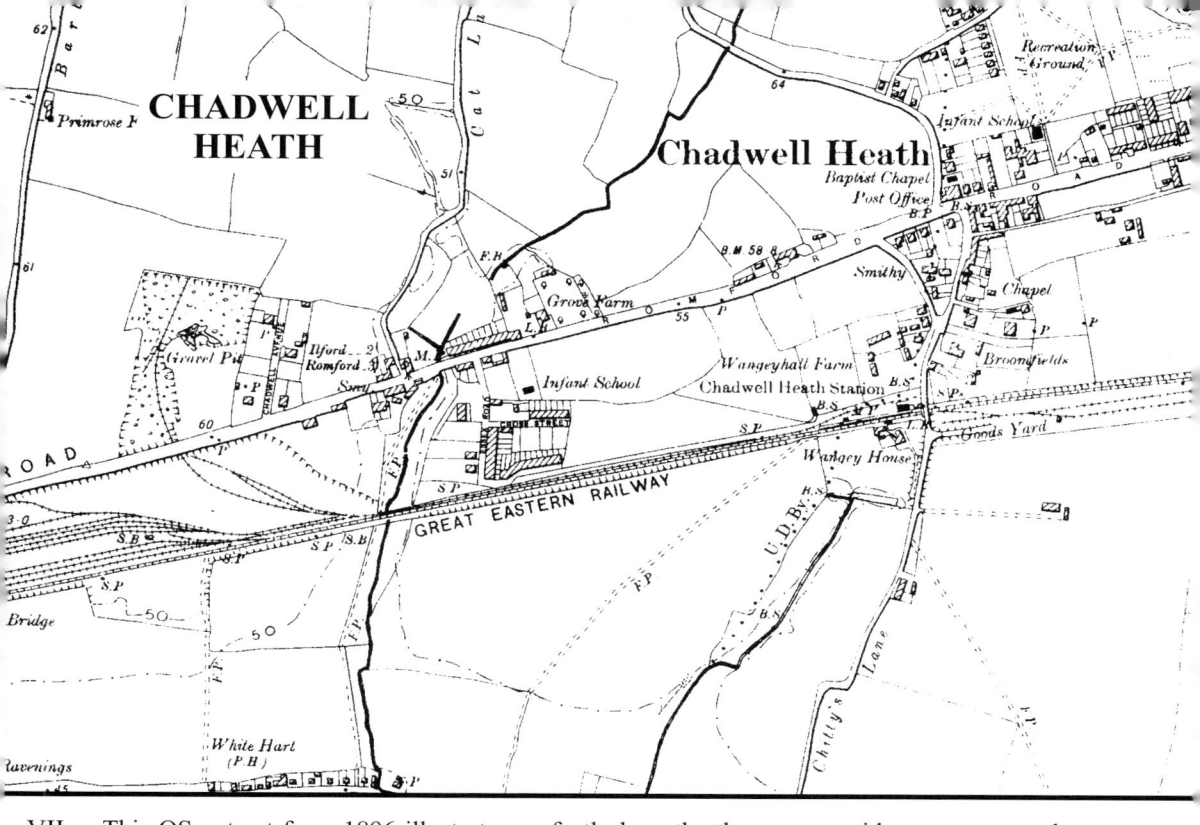

VII. This OS extract from 1896 illustrates perfectly how the then countryside gave way to the urban sprawl we have today. As the name implies, Chadwell Heath in GER days was largely surrounded by farmland. There were only two platforms until 1901.

31. Our view looking east shows the station in its original style with two platforms as built in 1864 by the GER. The building shown here, circa 1895, was demolished in 1900 to make way for the additional platforms. (Commercial postcard)

32. Here we witness Chadwell Heath after the 1901 widening to four platforms, showing the new ticket office above the tracks at street level, looking east from the London end in 1910. Exchange sidings for the London County Council Becontree estate railway latterly occupied the area of land to the right. (British Rail)

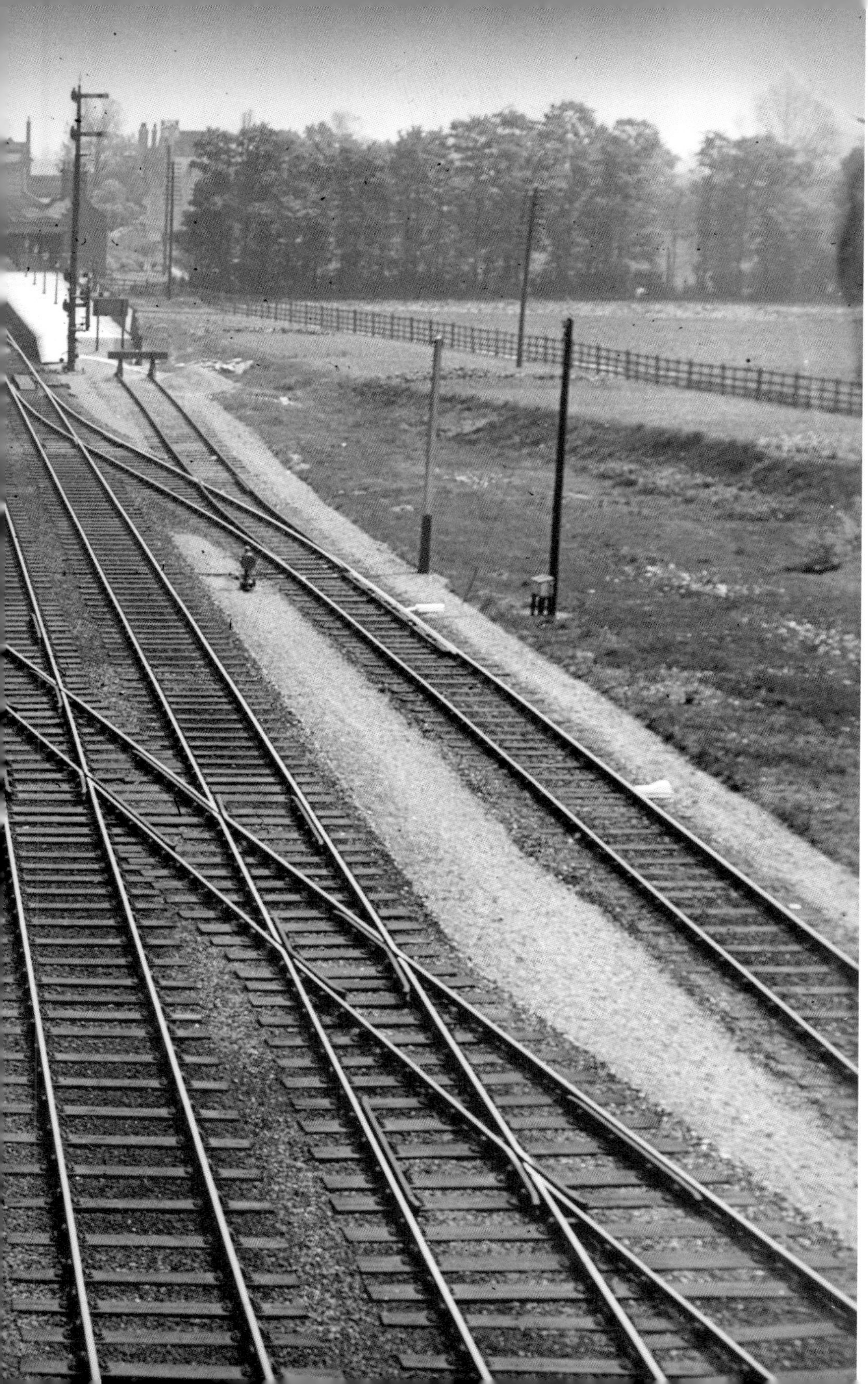

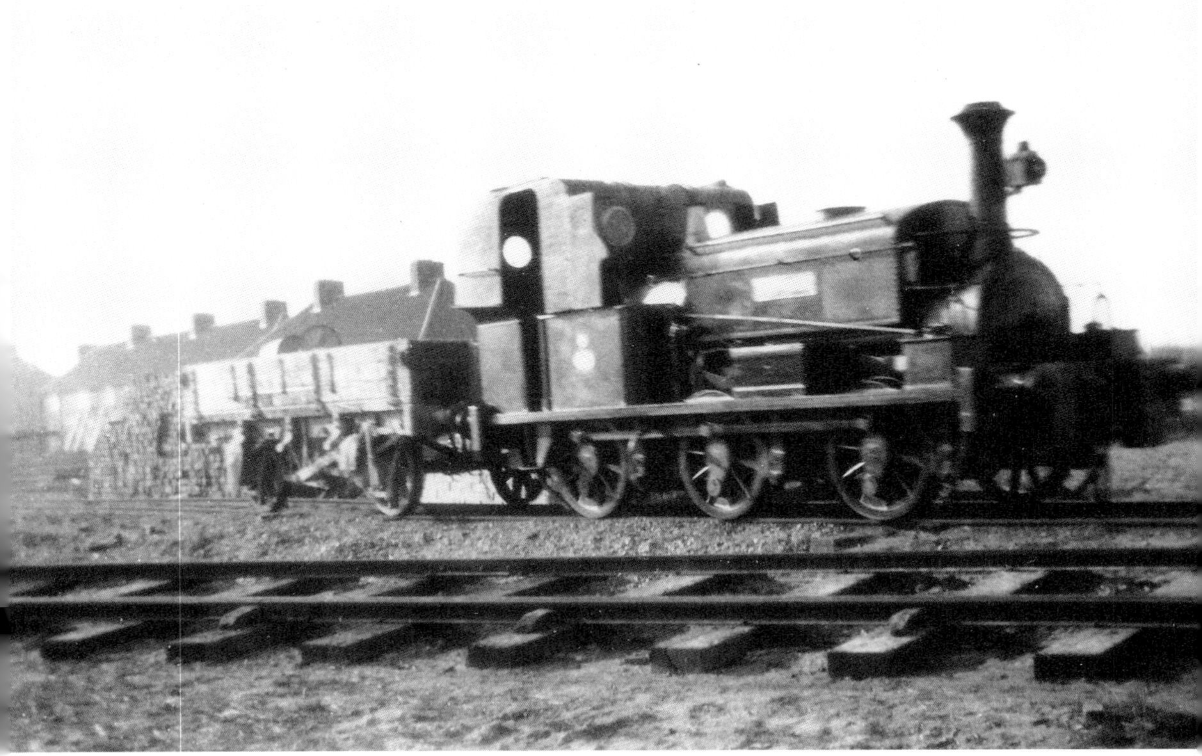

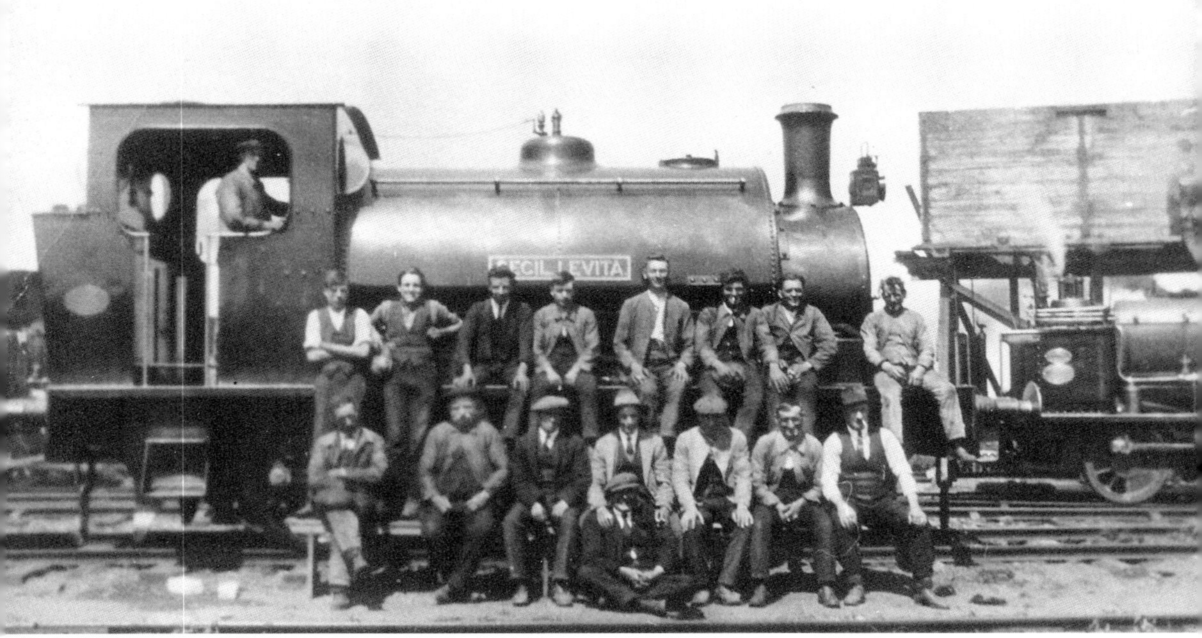
CECIL LEVITA

33. In 1921 the LCC embarked upon the Becontree estate which covered over 3000 acres. A temporary railway system was built to transport building materials around the site and ran for several miles down to a jetty on the River Thames via bridges over the LTSR lines. Over 600 wagons and 13 steam locomotives were used on the railway complex. Here we see one of the locomotives, 1876 Manning Wardle & Co 0-6-0ST no. 595 *Swansea,* running over the unballasted temporary estate railway in the 1920s. (G.Wells coll.)

34. This view is of the locomotive drivers and firemen employed on the Becontree estate railway. The locomotive, Hunslet 0-6-0T no. 1499 of 1926, was delivered new to the contractors, C.J. Wills in 1926 and was named *Cecil Lavita* after the chairman of the LCC Housing Committee. (G.Wells coll.)

35. This photo was taken from the same spot, but at a lower perspective than the 1910 picture (no. 32). LNER class L1 2-6-4 no. 9000 departs with the 12.50pm Gidea Park to Liverpool Street service on 3rd May 1947. (K.Nunn/LCGB)

36. Only three years have passed, but many changes have taken place. This strange sight is EM1 Bo-Bo electric no. 26002 hauling a Shenfield - Ilford Car Sheds test train at Chadwell Heath on 5th November 1950. (K.Nunn/LCGB)

37. Later that same day we see the same locomotive heading another test train through Chadwell Heath towards Shenfield. These later became class 76s and gave sterling service on the Manchester - Sheffield lines until their demise in 1981. (K.Nunn/LCGB)

38. Looking west we see the spectacle of the Ilford Car Sheds pilot No. 26510 on a regenerative braking test train with a 3x3-car class 306 train on 19th November 1950. This locomotive was withdrawn in 1964. (K.Nunn/LCGB)

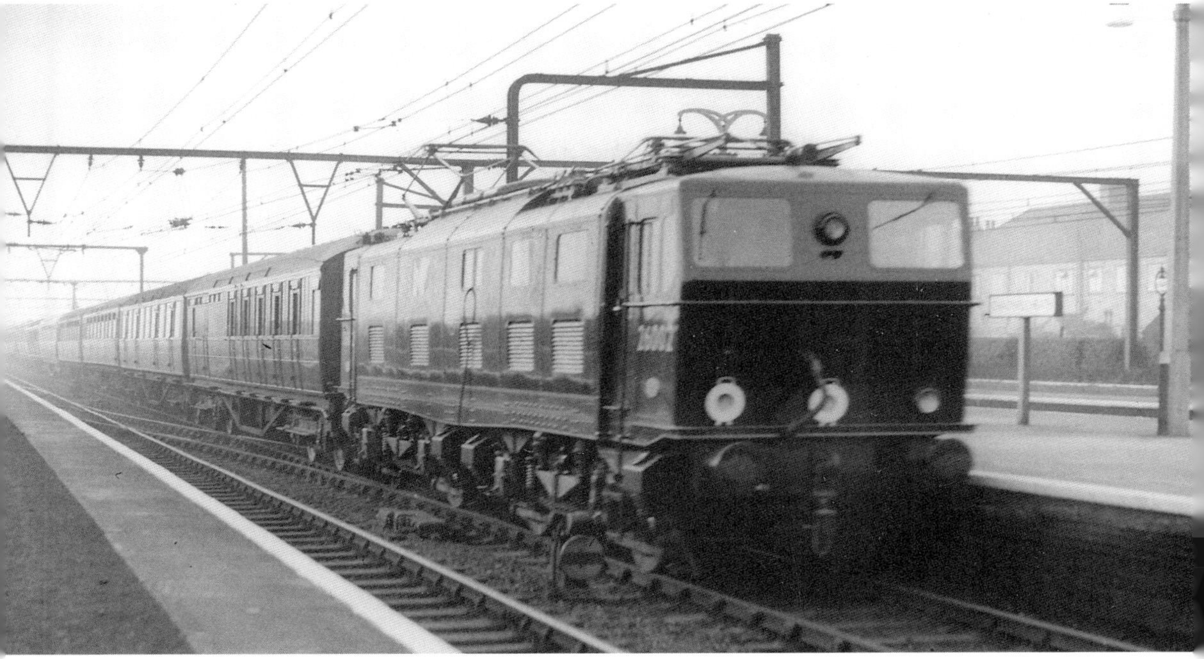

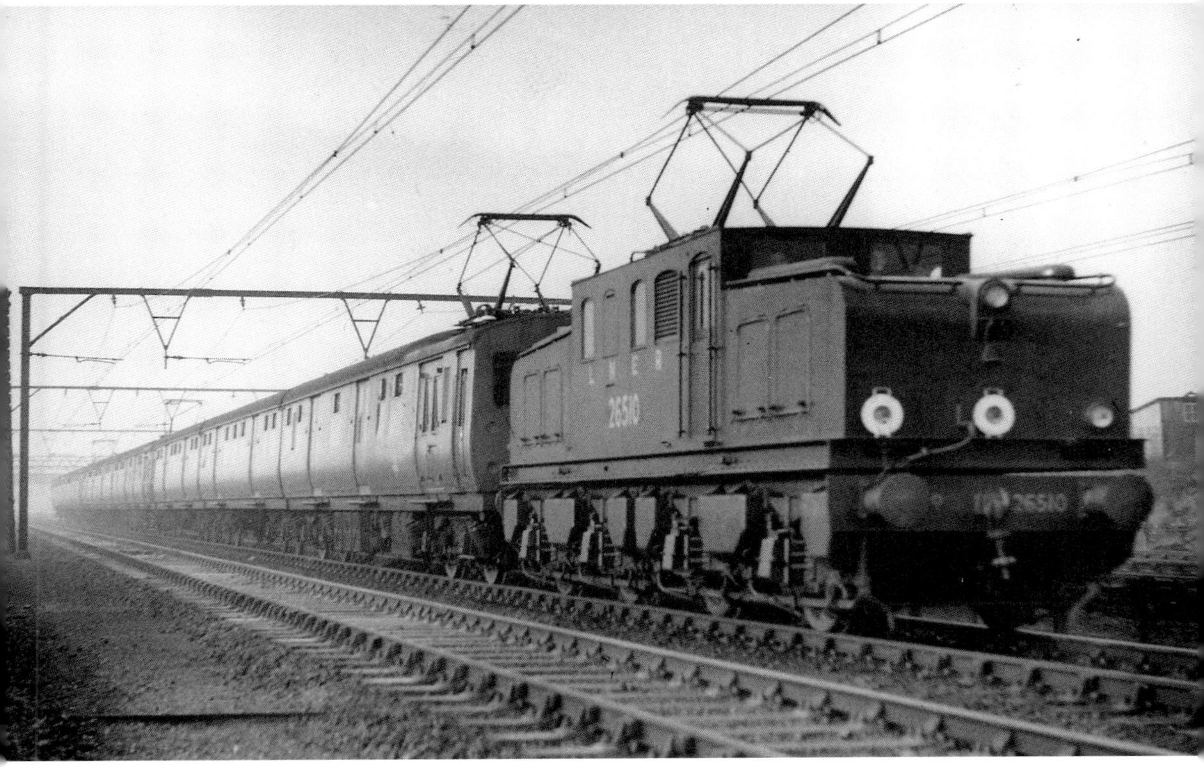
L N E R
26510
26510

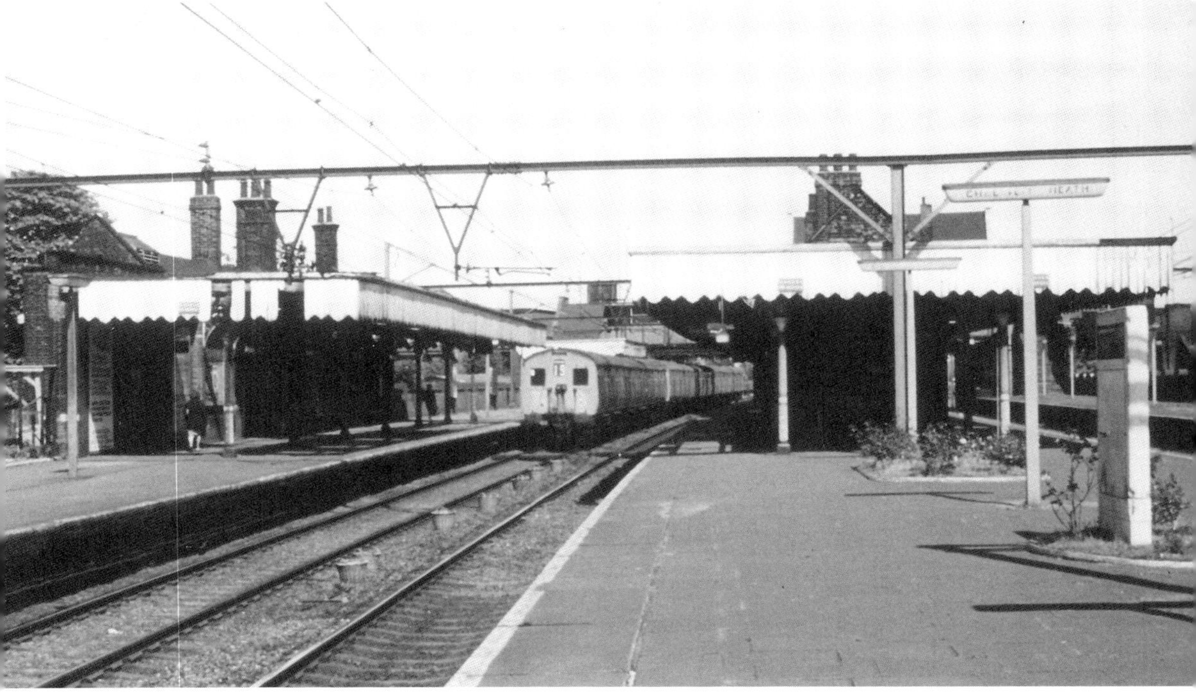

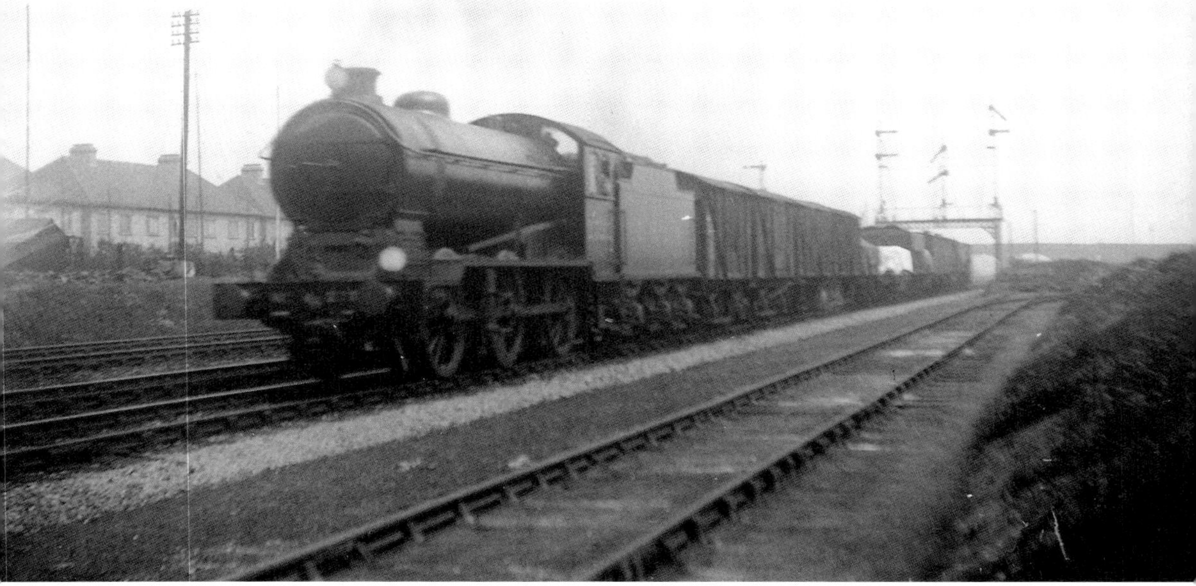

39. We now observe a class 306 9-car formation leaving on a Liverpool Street - Gidea Park service on 30th May 1974. (A.Young)

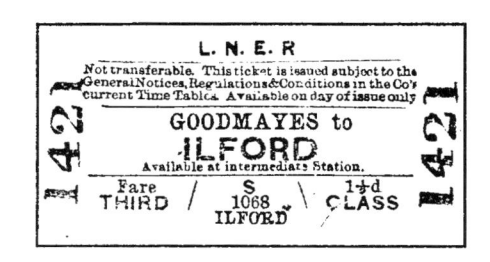

41. This is Chadwell Heath country end junction in September 1949 looking east. The siding curving away to the right formerly served William Boyer's gravel pit. The main line junction was removed during the 1997 resignalling programme. (British Rail)

40. Here we see LNER class J39 0-6-0 no. 2722 approaching Chadwell Heath with a Parkeston Quay to Spitalfields goods on 1st June 1929. We are looking east towards Whalebone Lane bridge in the distance. (K.Nunn/LCGB)

42. This sad sight was the former signal box in 1993, which had been out of use since 1972, when it was demoted to a relay room. Vandals had started the demolition of the box before contractors moved in during 1997. (J.Connor)

43. Looking west, we see Crowlands signal box (closed on 22nd May 1949) between Chadwell Heath and Romford on 9th September 1936. The GER planned a station here in 1900 and foundations were laid, but nothing further happened until the LNER 1935 electrification plan, which again promoted Crowlands station. The idea was dropped after WW2, but the platform foundations survive in the undergrowth. (British Rail)

WEST OF ROMFORD

44. Our view here is from Romford signal box looking west. The Gas Works can clearly be seen to dominate this area and a LNER J39 0-6-0 fusses about amongst the myriad of wagons on 16th September 1936. (British Rail)

```
GREAT EASTERN RAILWAY
Issued subject to Regulations in the
Company's Time Tables.
     GOODMAYES    to
Goodmayes                    Goodmayes
         STRATFORD
Stratford                    Stratford
        5d.   FARE   5d.
           Third Class
```
3180

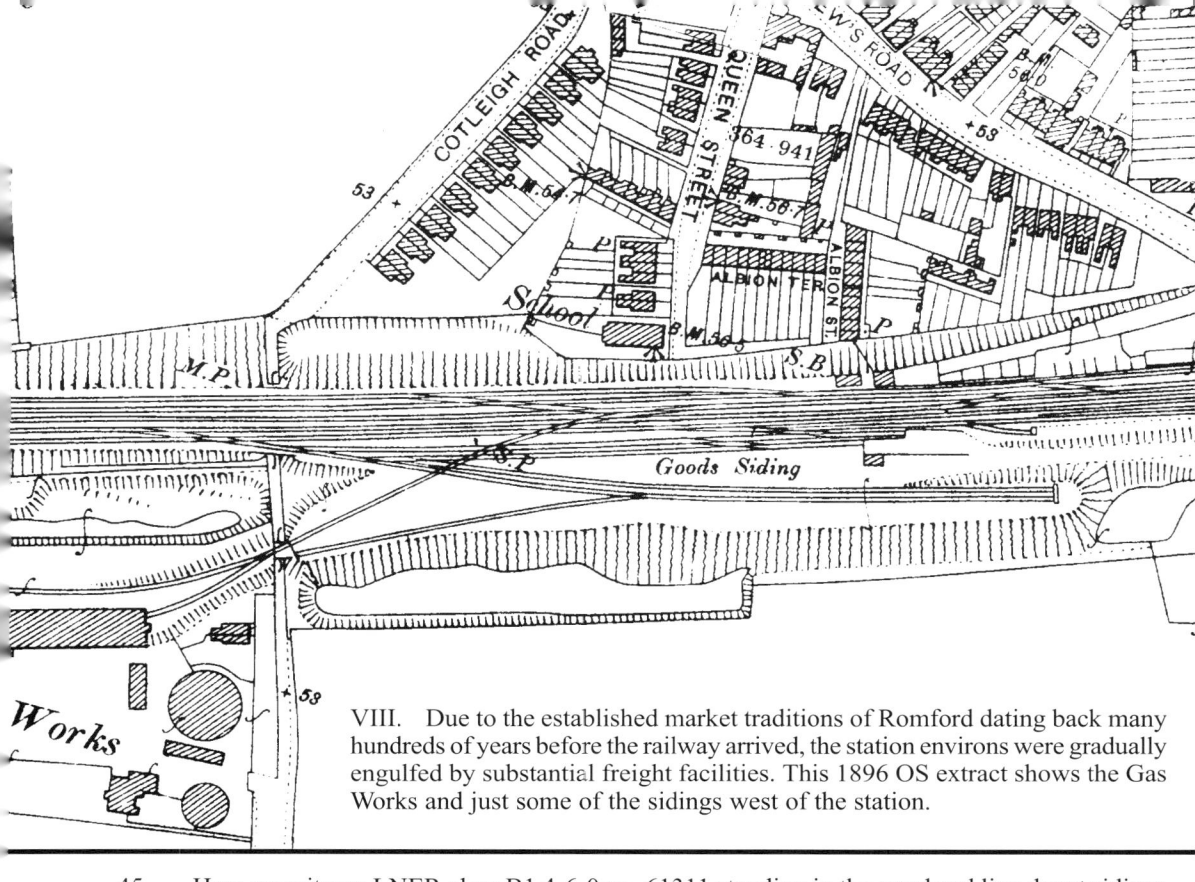

VIII. Due to the established market traditions of Romford dating back many hundreds of years before the railway arrived, the station environs were gradually engulfed by substantial freight facilities. This 1896 OS extract shows the Gas Works and just some of the sidings west of the station.

45. Here we witness LNER class B1 4-6-0 no. 61311 standing in the overhead line depot sidings on a wiring train. An L1 2-6-4 can be glimpsed behind the B1. This view was taken in 1960 and by 1962 steam had been banished from East Anglia. Until the early 1990s one could see former LNER coaches in the formation of 'Wiring Trains' standing in these sidings. (G.Wells)

ROMFORD

46. We look west as a St. Albans to Clacton excursion thunders through, hauled by GER class Y14 (LNER J15) 0-6-0 no. 642. Gas lighting, enamel adverts and various items of station furniture adorn this pure Victorian scene although taken on 2nd July 1910. (K.Nunn/LCGB)

47. Looking east we have an overall view of the busy goods sidings with cattle facilities next to the signal box and a water tower for thirsty locomotives opposite. The station lies in the distance in this 1911 image. (British Rail)

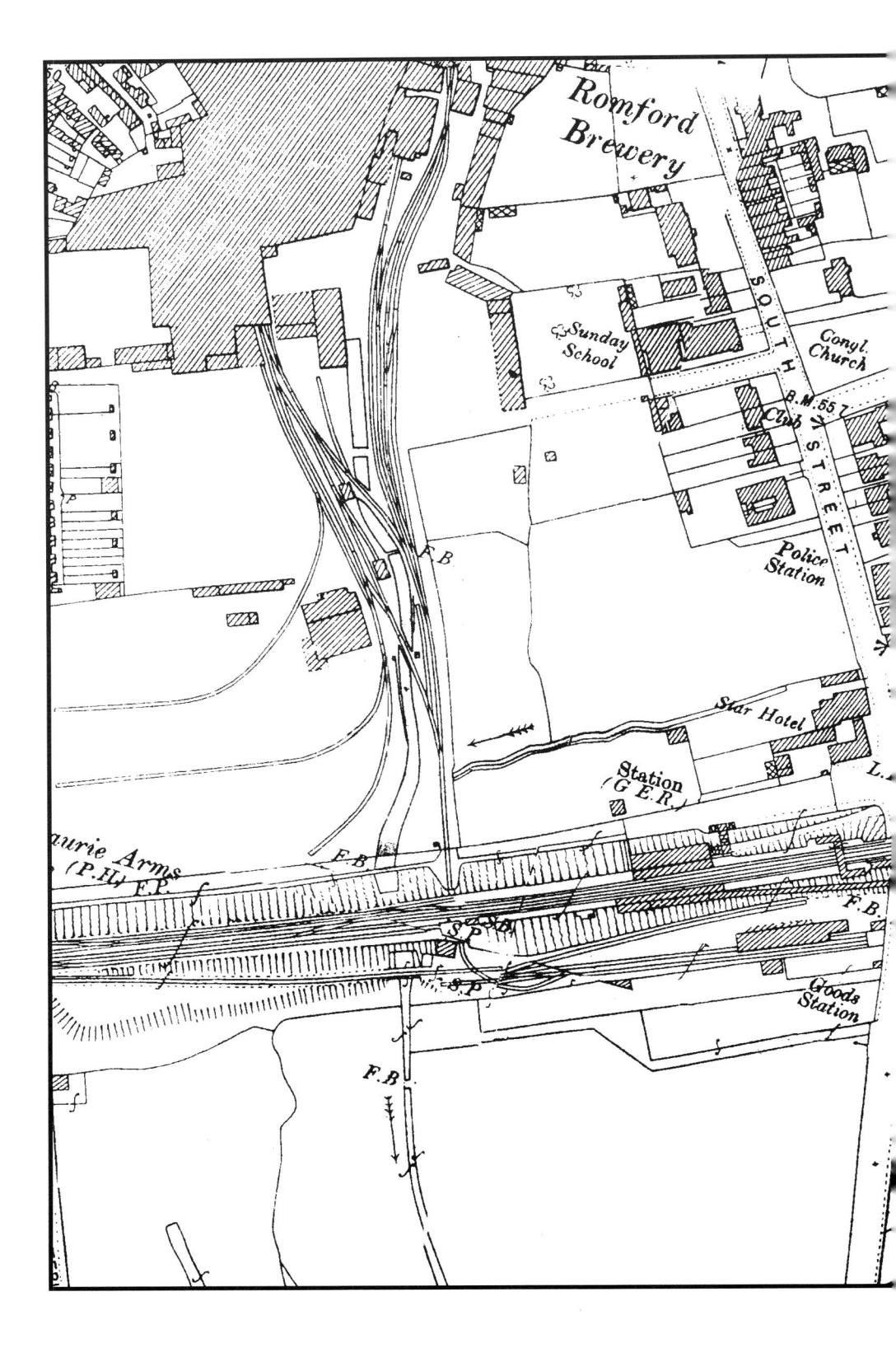

Romford
Brewery

Sunday
School

Congl.
Church

B.M.55.7

Club

SOUTH STREET

Police
Station

Star Hotel

Station
(G.E.R.)

aurie Arms
(P.H.) F.P.

F.B.

F.B.

S.P.

S.P.

Goods
Station

F.B.

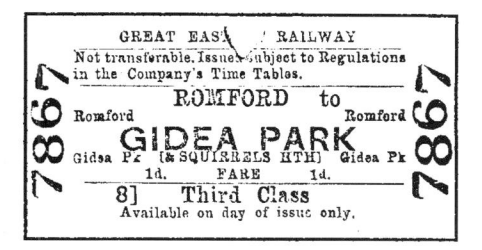

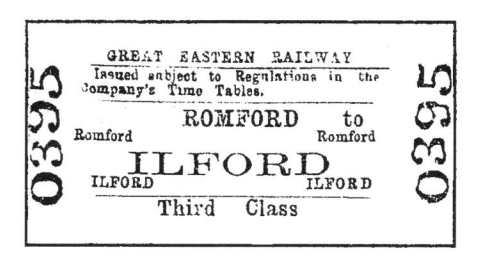

IX. Romford station dates back to the opening of the line on 20th June 1839. Originally built as an island platform, it was improved with conventional side platforms in 1860. The separate LTSR station opened on 7th June 1893 on the opposite side of South Street. This OS map from 1896 shows the stations in their original form and the extensive sidings built to cope with the traffic from Romford Brewery.

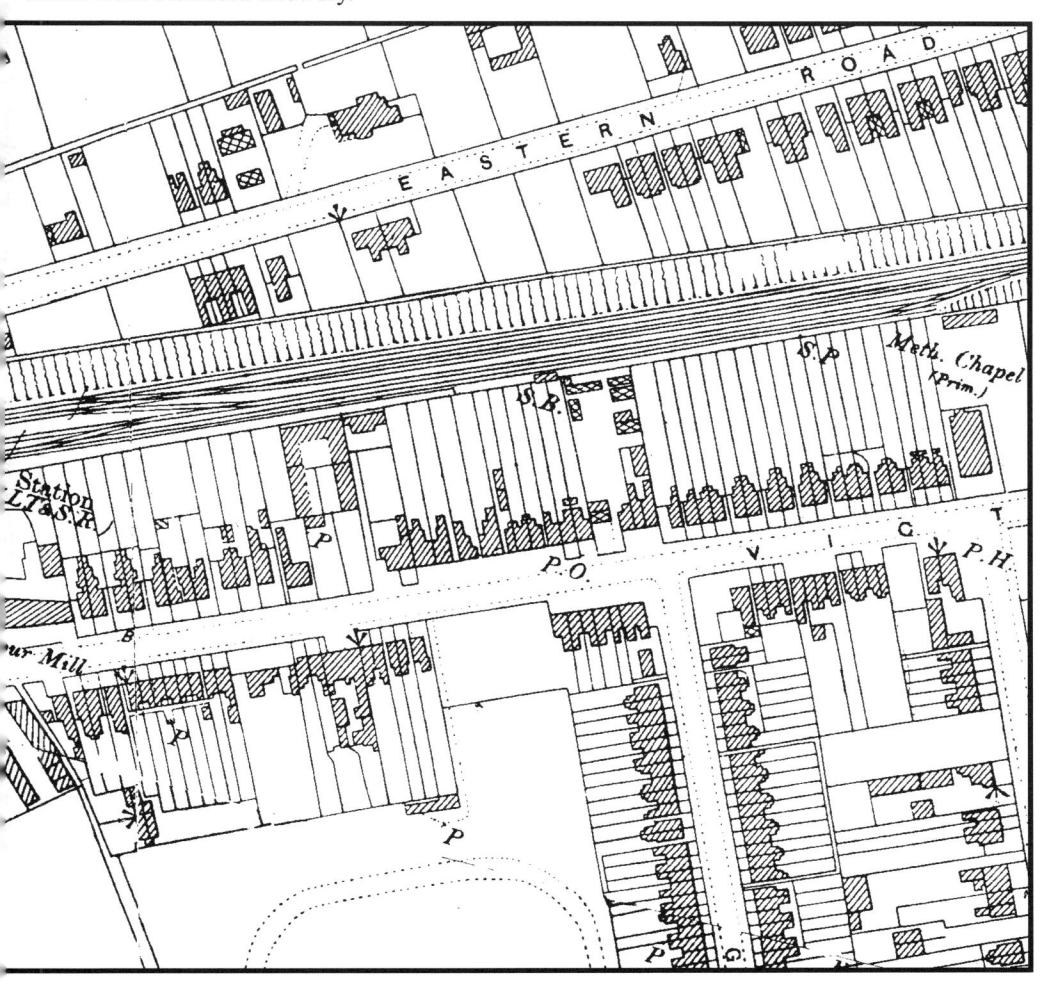

48. Romford's lower goods yard was reached by a notoriously difficult incline, which caused several hair-raising incidents for the engine drivers. All the wagons for the brewery would be assembled here before being taken under the main line via a tunnel into the brewery on the left. An engine can be seen heading towards the tunnel, which, after many years of disuse, has amazingly survived. (British Rail)

49. The hazardous nature of the lower yard at Romford is exemplified by this GER view of 1911. One would hope that the wagons were attached to a locomotive as they roll into the yard, as shortly beyond the buffer stops is South Street! (British Rail)

50. Access to the brewery was first by a wagon hoist and a small turntable, until the tunnel was opened in the 1860s via this very sharp curve in the lower yard. Ind Coope owned two steam locomotives for shunting wagons in their yard. (British Rail)

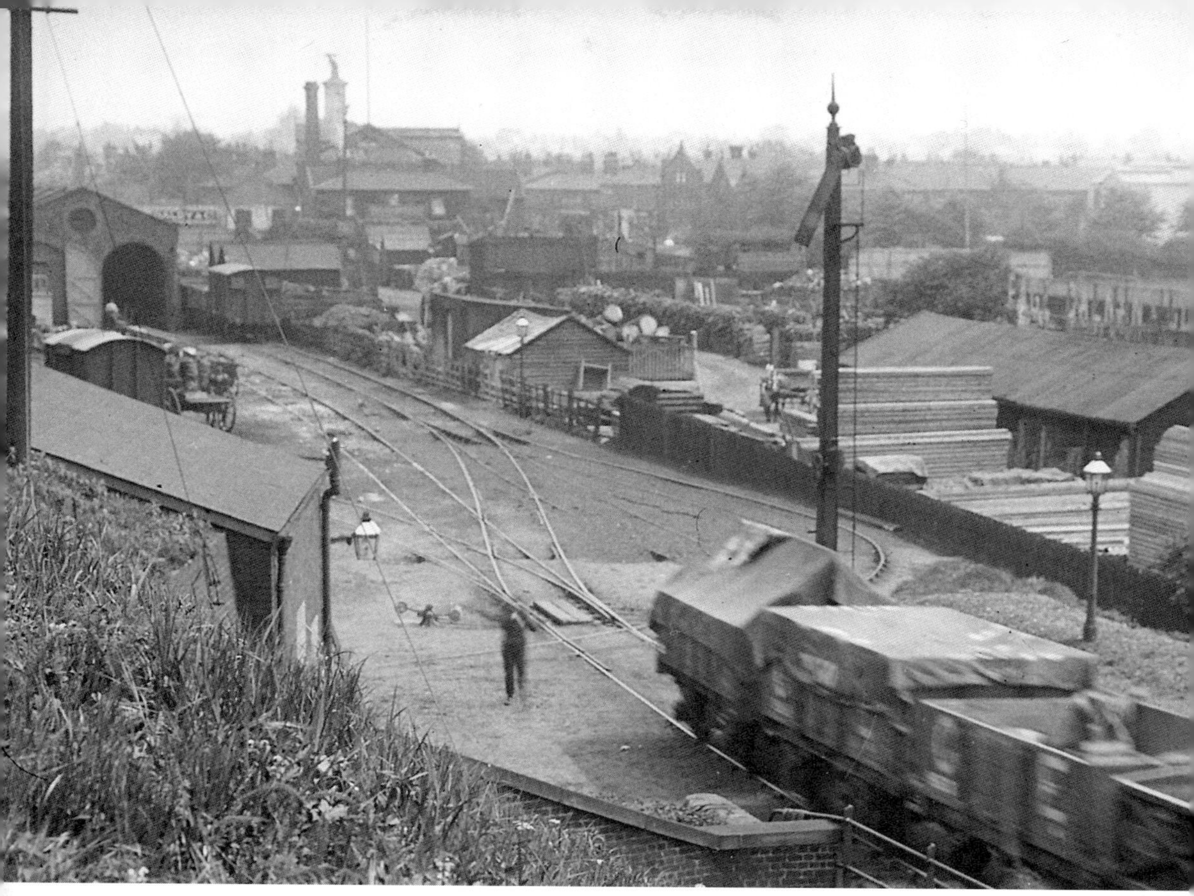

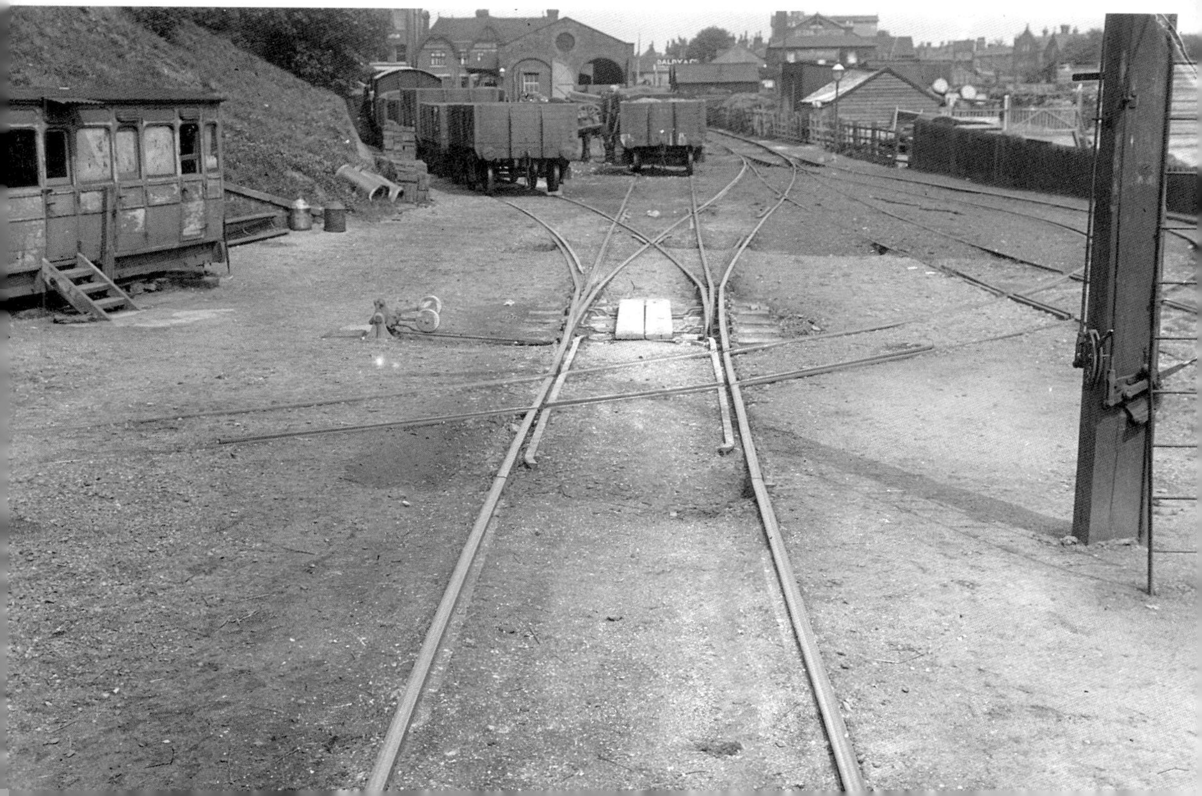

51. The London Tilbury & Southend Railway opened their Romford station on 7th June 1893. We see the original station in this 1911 view looking east. The entrance in South Street closed on 1st April 1934, and passengers subsequently accessed the platform via the footbridge from the LNER station. (British Rail)

52. This view taken from the north side of the line shows the down platform entrance just as preparation for the widening work is about to commence on 2nd March 1930. Evocative LNER signs and posters abound as passers-by look on. (British Rail)

53. The vast amounts of earth needed for the widening and the upheaval encountered can be appreciated in this view from Romford signal box on 28th May 1930. Beyond the cattle pens (note the steep incline), wagons of earth are being unloaded to form the new embankment. (R.R.Clow/ Harwich Shipping & Railway Museum)

GO.SLOW

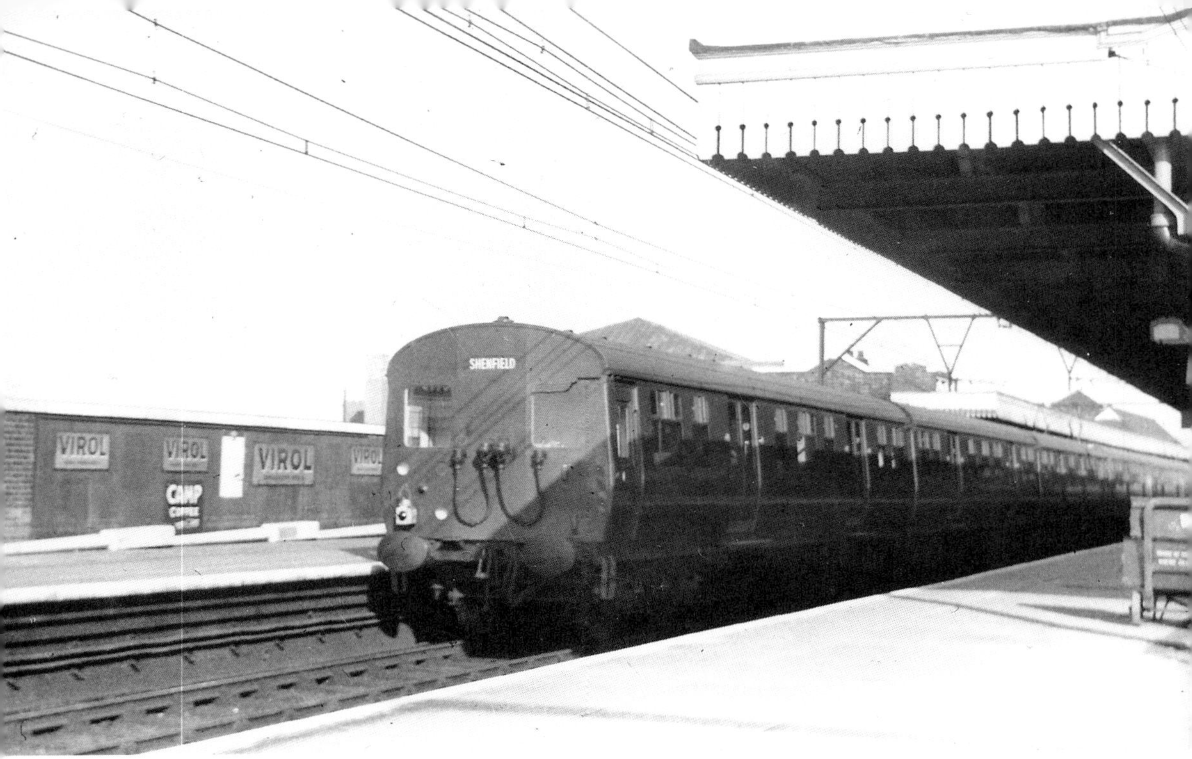
SHENFIELD
VIROL
VIROL
VIROL
VIROL
CAMP
COFFEE

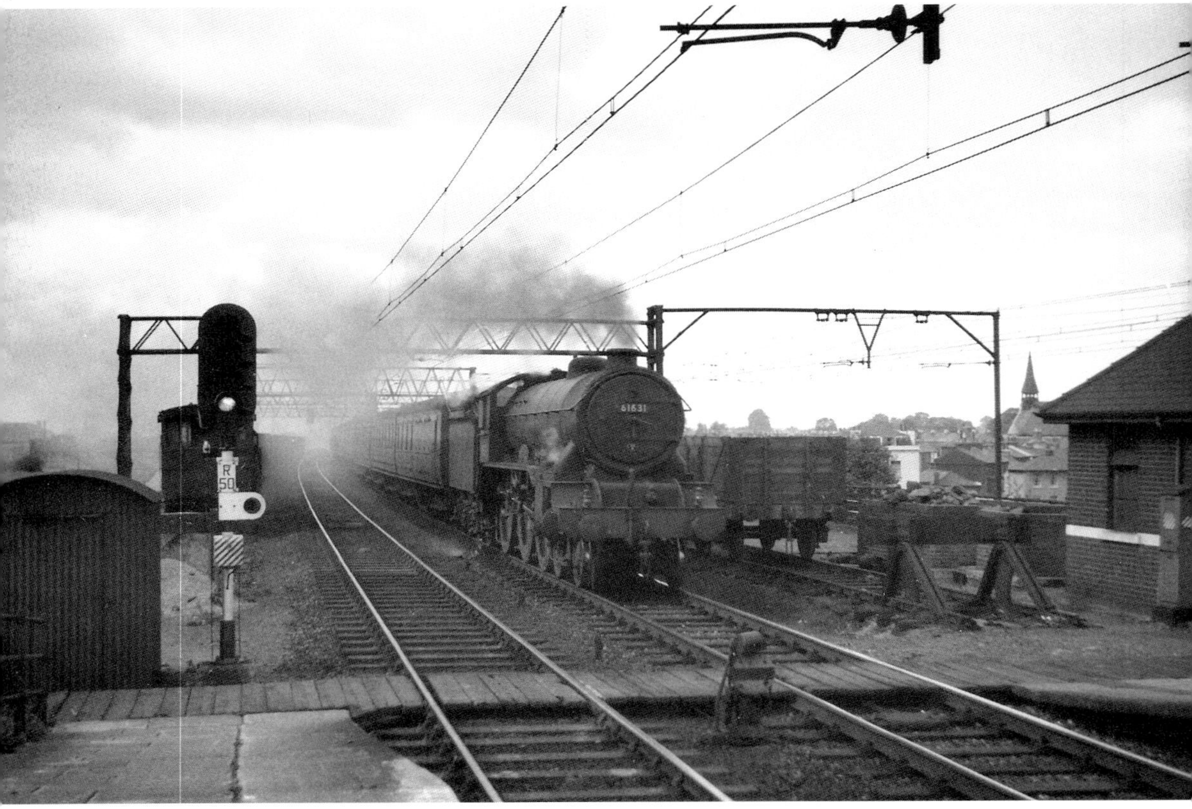
61631
R
50

54. A Liverpool Street - Shenfield train formed of new class 306 units is shown leaving in 1949. In contrast, the Southend service was steam hauled until 1956, giving passengers a choice of traction from both ends of the spectrum. (A.C.Ingram)

55. Steam under the wires approaching Romford. A Liverpool Street - Southend Victoria service hauled by LNER class B17 4-6-0 no. 61631 *Serlby Hall* enters the station on 19th August 1952. (Kidderminster Railway Museum)

56. Here we see another B17, no. 61664 *Liverpool*, as she thunders through Romford with a London bound express on 19th August 1952. Unlike many other stations on this section, Romford has retained many original features, including the canopies.
(Kidderminster Railway Museum)

The Upminster branch is illustrated in the Middleton Press *Tilbury Loop* album.

57. The characteristic wooden platform of the Upminster branch platform at Romford is shown here as Midland Railway class 1P 0-4-4T no. 58062 of Plaistow shed prepares to leave in this early 1950s image. DMUs took over services on the branch from 1956 until electrification in 1986. (R.J.Buckley)

58. The centenary of the LTSR Upminster - Romford line took place on 5th June 1993, and here we can enjoy the preserved class 306 unit no. 017 leaving with a shuttle service to Upminster on the Centenary Gala Day. (D.Brennand)

GIDEA PARK

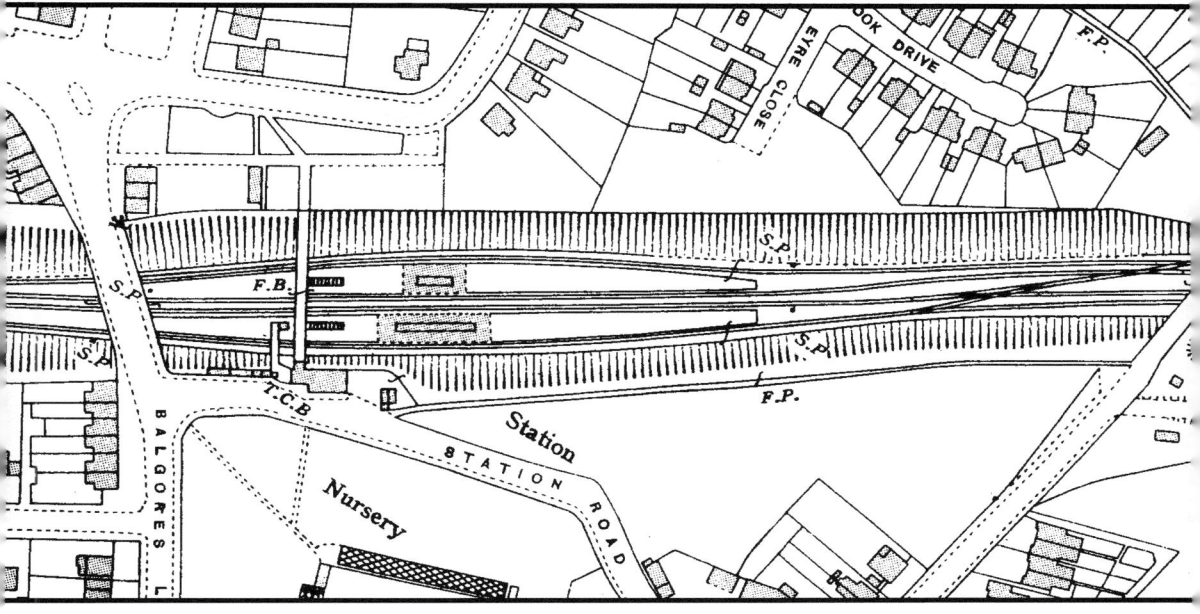

X. The station opened on 1st December 1910 as Squirrels Heath & Gidea Park, which only lasted three years, as from 1st October 1913 it became Gidea Park & Squirrels Heath. BR decided to drop '& Squirrels Heath' from 20th February 1969. This OS map from 1939 shows the station unaltered from the original plan of two island platforms.

59. Considerable widening work took place at Gidea Park to accommodate the station as seen in this view of the construction site looking east on 3rd April 1910. GER class M15 2-4-2T no. 177 works a Chelmsford to Liverpool Street service. (K.Nunn/LCGB)

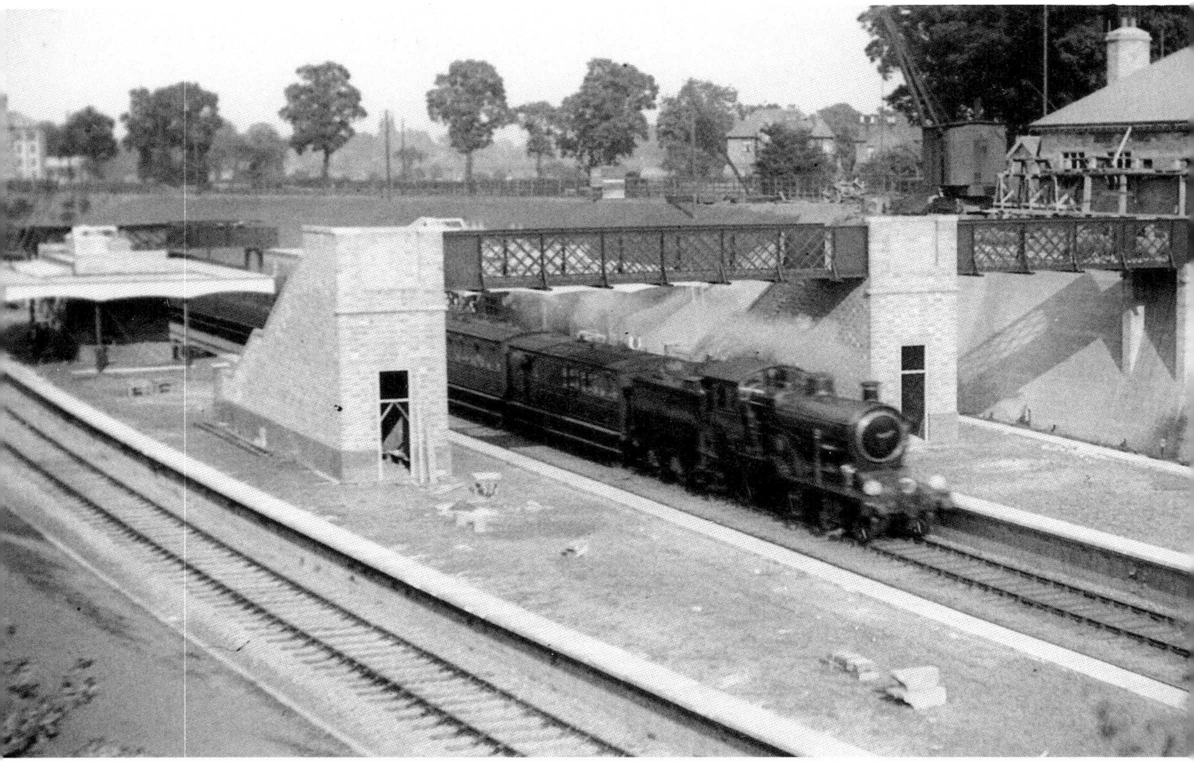

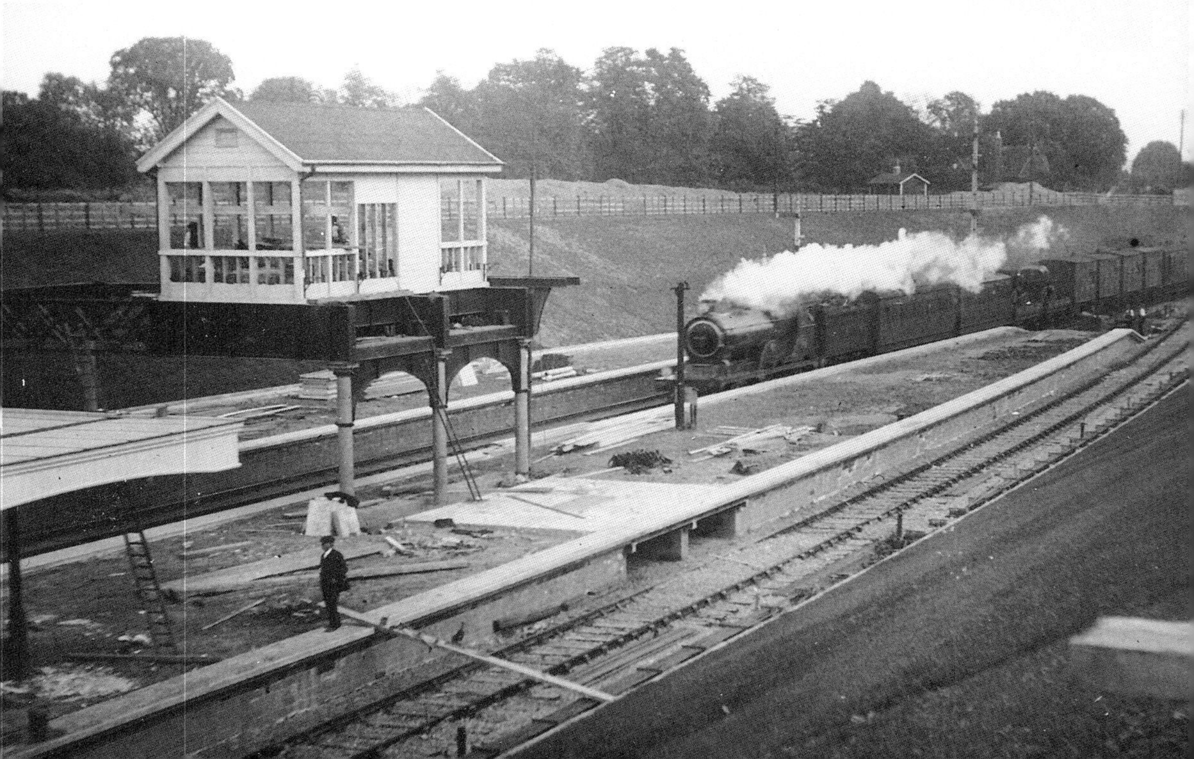

60. Just three months to go before opening, and we see GER 'Claud' class D56 4-4-0 no. 1818 heading towards London with a Yarmouth to Liverpool Street service on 3rd September 1910. Much of the station retains the original features, but the brick supports for the footbridge have been replaced by ironwork. (K.Nunn/LCGB)

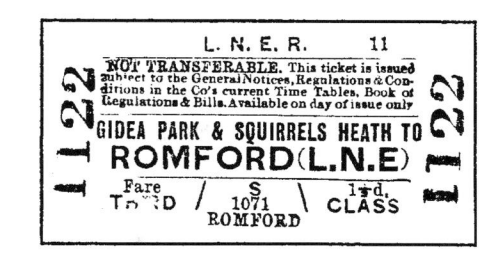

61. The siting of the signal box was unusual but practical from the signalman's viewpoint. GER 'Claud' class D56 4-4-0 no. 1816 heads towards London during the building stage on a mixed train from Ipswich on 19th September 1910. (K.Nunn/LCGB)

62. The big day has arrived at Squirrels Heath & Gidea Park, and our view is looking west on the first day of public opening, a rather damp 1st December 1910. Several of the station staff are posing on the signal box veranda. Beautifully manicured embankments and surrounding open spaces were destined not to last. (LNER)

63. The main line narrowed back to two tracks beyond Gidea Park as can be seen shortly after opening. The line on the left going under the new section of bridge leads into the sidings. Just beyond the bridge is the Romford Factory. (British Rail)

64. Looking west, we witness a LNER L1 class 2-6-4 no. 67723 approaching with a Liverpool Street to Shenfield service on 5th October 1949. The electric units had started running the previous month, but steam could not be dispensed with that quickly and therefore supplemented the service. (K.Nunn/LCGB)

65. On the same day as the previous picture we see a 9-car 306 formation leaving Gidea Park on its journey to Liverpool Street. These units were modified for AC voltage use between 1959 and 1960. The pantographs and guards compartments were resited to the middle coach at that time. (K.Nunn/LCGB)

66. Our view is from the footpath on the south side of the line, as we are treated to the spectacle of a trio of light engines heading towards Stratford depot on 17th August 1952. Class J15 0-6-0 no. 65476 leads, coupled to B17 4-6-0 no. 61648 *Arsenal,* with J17 0-6-0 no. 65563 at the rear. (Kidderminster Railway Museum)

ROMFORD FACTORY

67. Looking east from Upper Brentwood Road bridge in 1911 we have a good view of the simple run-round facility behind the signal box. The tall building on the right is the Romford Factory, whilst nearest the camera is the goods shed. Open space to the north of the line is devoid of any kind of dwelling. (British Rail)

68. Standing outside the Romford Factory signal box is GER class Y14 (later LNER J15) 0-6-0 no. 881 on a train used for the construction of Gidea Park station, which lies just beyond the overbridge. The building is the Provender Store, which was destroyed by fire in the 1960s. Our view west is dated 28th August 1910. (K.Nunn/LCGB)

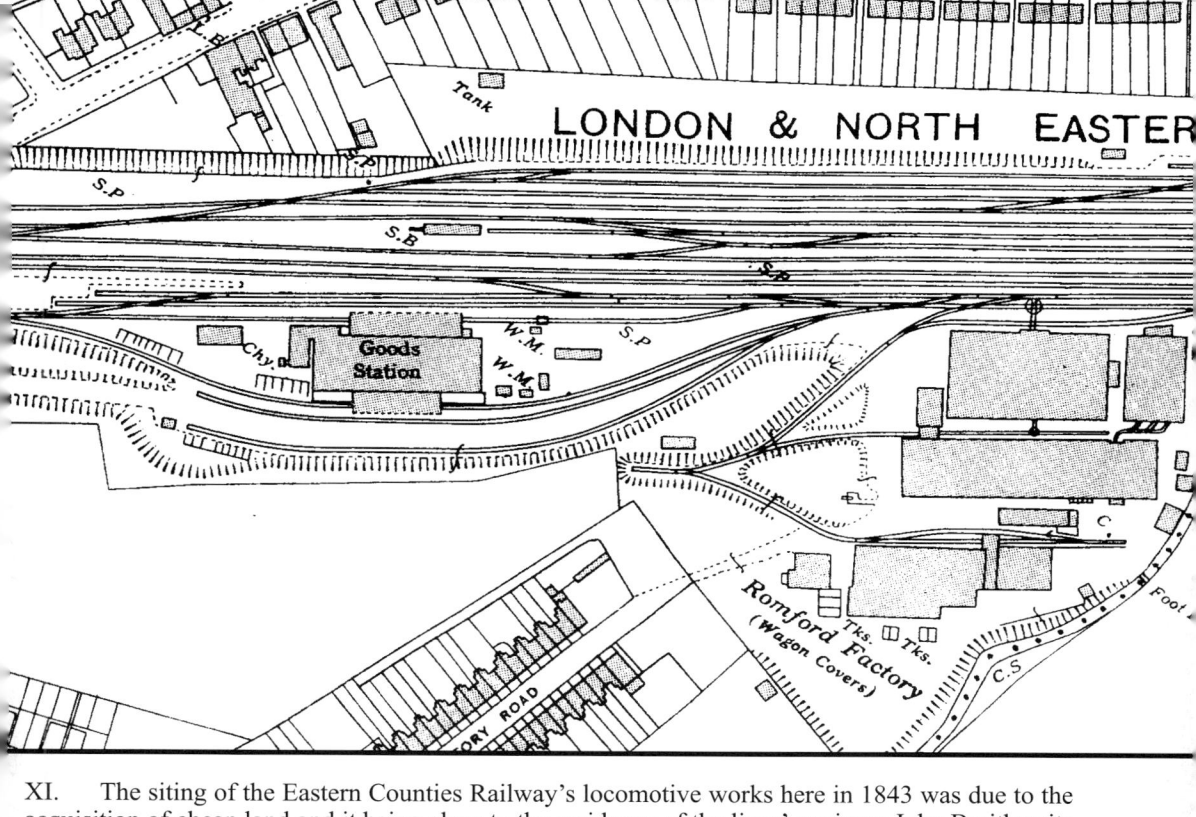

XI. The siting of the Eastern Counties Railway's locomotive works here in 1843 was due to the acquisition of cheap land and it being close to the residence of the lines' engineer John Braithwaite at nearby Hare Hall, rather than practical considerations. The title stems from Romford being the nearest station in 1843. The transfer of locomotive construction to Stratford in 1847 left the factory in a state of limbo, until about 1854, when a decision was taken to use the building for making wagon sheets. This 1939 OS map shows the site after the 1930s widening.

69. Additional carriage sidings were laid during the widening as we look east on 3rd February 1932. Also added was this much larger signal box which had opened the previous year replacing Romford Factory box to the east. The box shown here survived until the 1997 resignalling and was demolished shortly afterwards. (British Rail)

70. A feature of the Romford Factory is this central archway, being the entrance for locomotives via a small turntable outside the building. The buildings have Grade II listed status and are destined to become part of a residential estate. (D.Brennand)

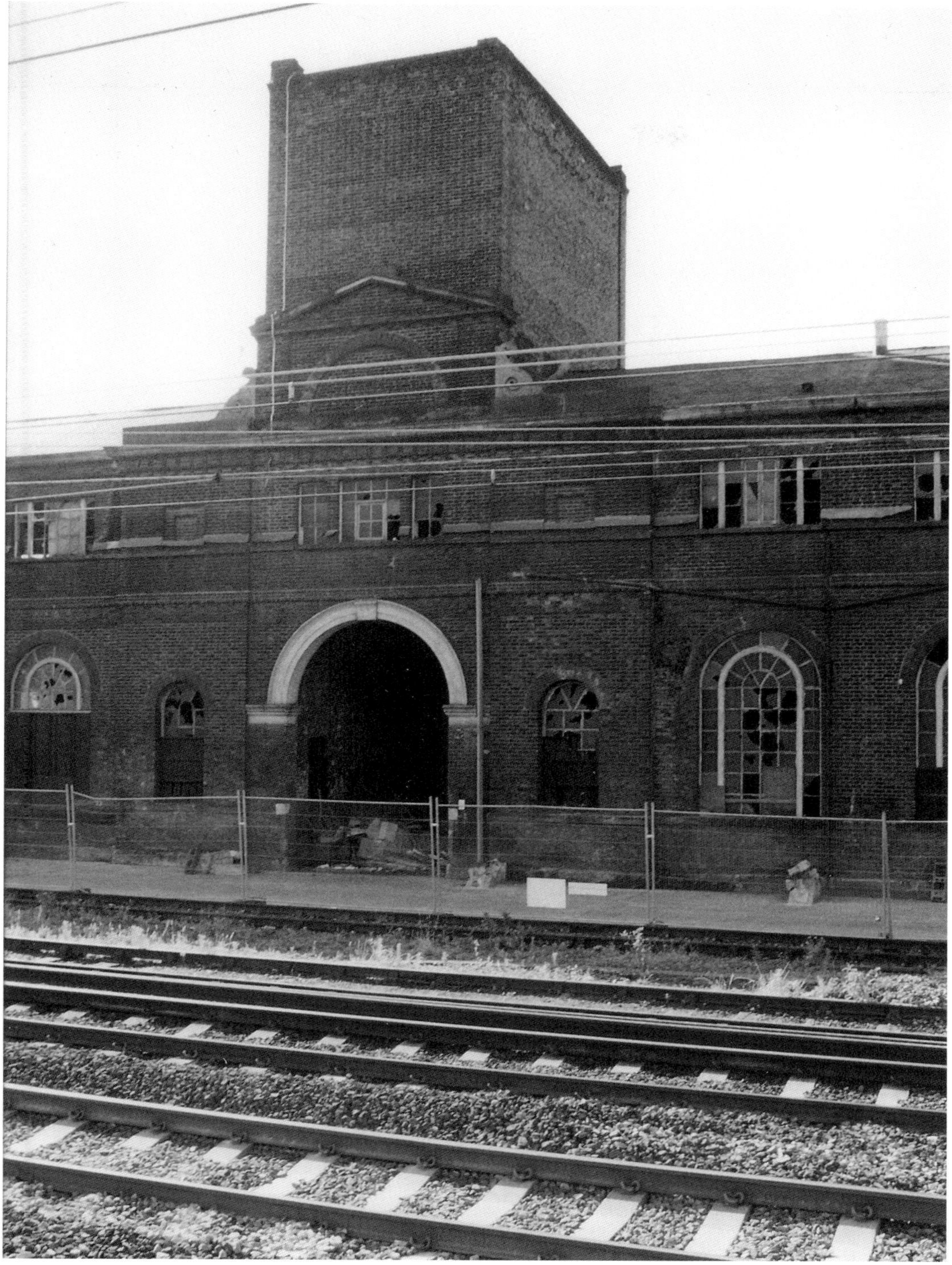

71. Our view here is of the rear of the Romford Factory showing the boiler house during redevelopment work in September 2001. The building retained a surprisingly large number of original architectural features at this time. (D.Brennand)

72. On the 30th June 2002, a terrible fire caused considerable damage to the main building, as seen here the next day. The roof has collapsed and virtually all the internal timber has been burnt away leaving an almost empty shell. The brickwork looks remarkably intact, but there was consternation that the tower would collapse. Despite the fire, the redevelopment of the site carried on. (D.Brennand)

HAROLD WOOD

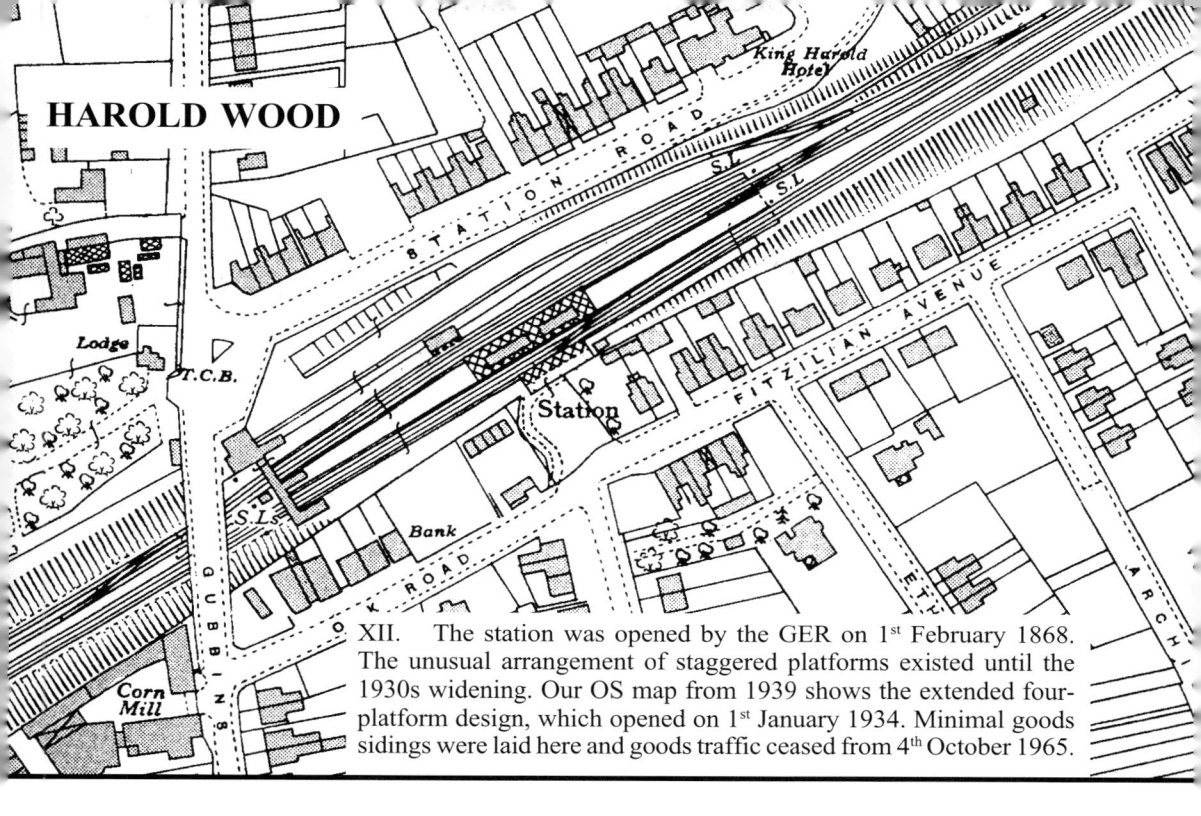

XII. The station was opened by the GER on 1st February 1868. The unusual arrangement of staggered platforms existed until the 1930s widening. Our OS map from 1939 shows the extended four-platform design, which opened on 1st January 1934. Minimal goods sidings were laid here and goods traffic ceased from 4th October 1965.

73. Here we see the wooden platforms of Harold Wood in 1910 looking east. The signal box became redundant during the 1930s widening when colour light signalling was installed, controlled from Gidea Park and Brentwood boxes. (J.E.Connor coll.)

HAROLD WOOD

74. Looking east from Gubbins Lane we see the offset platforms of Harold Wood in this 1931 view. Horses and carts await their loads in the small goods yard. A further long siding ran behind the signal box to serve a brickworks. (J.E.Connor coll.)

75. The extent of the widening can be appreciated in this view, looking east on 15th July 1939. Passengers wait on the London bound main line platform, which subsequently lost its canopy, but the others have survived. (H.C.Casserley)

76. LNER class N7 0-6-2 no. 471 departs with a Shenfield - Liverpool Street service formed of Gresley quad-art stock, on 15th July 1939. These sets had five bogies under four bodies, a system re-invented for Eurostar trains. (H.C.Casserley)

77. The station gained this new ticket office and entrance hall during the 1930s widening programme. Looking west, we see LNER class B17/1 4-6-0 no. 2804 *Elveden* arriving with a Liverpool Street - Southend Victoria service on 15th July 1939. The LNER signs contrast nicely with the former GER benches. (H.C.Casserley)

78. Over sixty years have elapsed since the previous picture, and due to the efforts of First Great Eastern, we can again witness the spectacle of steam over this historic line. LMS 'Black Five' 4-6-0 no. 45157 *Glasgow Highlander* heads 'The Lifeboat Express' from Liverpool Street to Harwich on 5th May 2002. (D.Brennand)

79. This view of the station entrance could have easily been taken in the 1930s, except for the Nat West cash-point and obligatory graffiti, which date the photograph firmly in the present century, on 5th May 2002. The legend LNER, covered up for many years during British Rail days, has subsequently been revealed once more. (D.Brennand)

45157
2
3

LNER HAROLD WOOD LNER
NatWest
Oak Road
Shops and Services
Station Road Shops
Library
Station Car Park

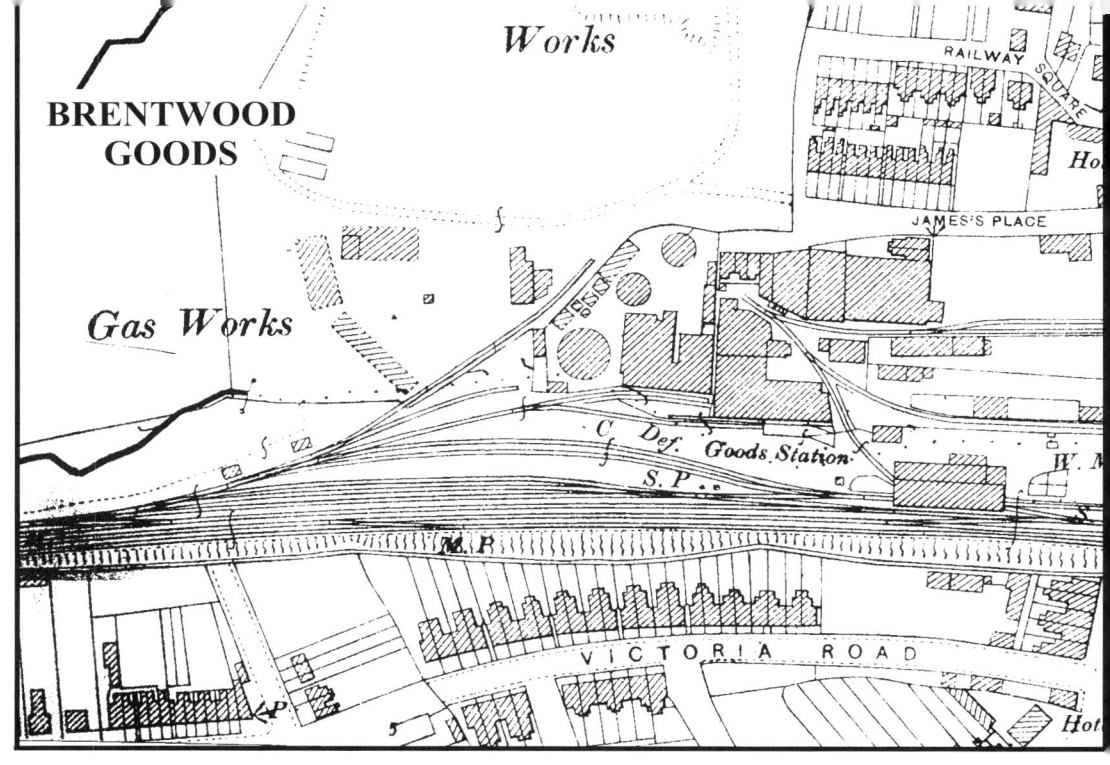

XIII. Numerous businesses evolved around the goods yard at Brentwood. Our OS map of 1896 shows this to good effect. Thomas Moy, London Co-Op and North Thames Gas Board were just a few of the companies using the yard.

80. Our view here, looking north east, is of GER class C32 2-4-2 no. 1087 on a breakdown train in Brentwood yard. Various structures give an industrious backdrop to this scene, recorded on 26th May 1911. (K.Nunn/LCGB)

81.   Hauling what appear to be brand new 6-wheel coaches from Stratford Works to Felixstowe, is GER class Y14 (LNER J15) 0-6-0 no. 555. It is heading east up Brentwood incline and is passing the goods yard on 19th August 1912. (K.Nunn/LCGB)

82.   Looking east we witness GER class T19 2-4-0 no. 1034 hurtling down Brentwood bank with a Parkeston Quay to Liverpool Street train on 11th May 1913. The houses on the right of the picture have survived, thereby providing a perfect reference point. By good fortune, our photographer lived in Brentwood for many years. (K.Nunn/LCGB)

83. At the country end of the goods yard was the cattle dock. The cattlemen would have had a difficult task driving the beasts up the steep hill to Brentwood market. Just beyond the bridge is Brentwood station, where we see milk churns awaiting collection on the platform in this circa 1912 view. (British Rail)

84. During the 1930s widening programme, this elaborate four storey signal box was erected opposite Brentwood yard. The elevated position was deemed necessary to give the signalmen a panoramic view over the yard and main lines. Our picture is dated 26th June 1934. The signal box was given a reinforced brick base during WW2 for added strength. The box was taken out of use on 28th November 1971, but the brick base still stands today. (R. R.Clow/Harwich Shipping & Railway Museum)

85. Brentwood yard, along with Ware in Hertfordshire, were two locations where these rather odd looking LNER class Y11 4-wheel petrol shunting locomotives could be found. Here we see no. 8188 standing next to Brentwood cattle dock on 17th April 1948. The goods yard closed on 7th December 1970. (K.Nunn/LCGB)

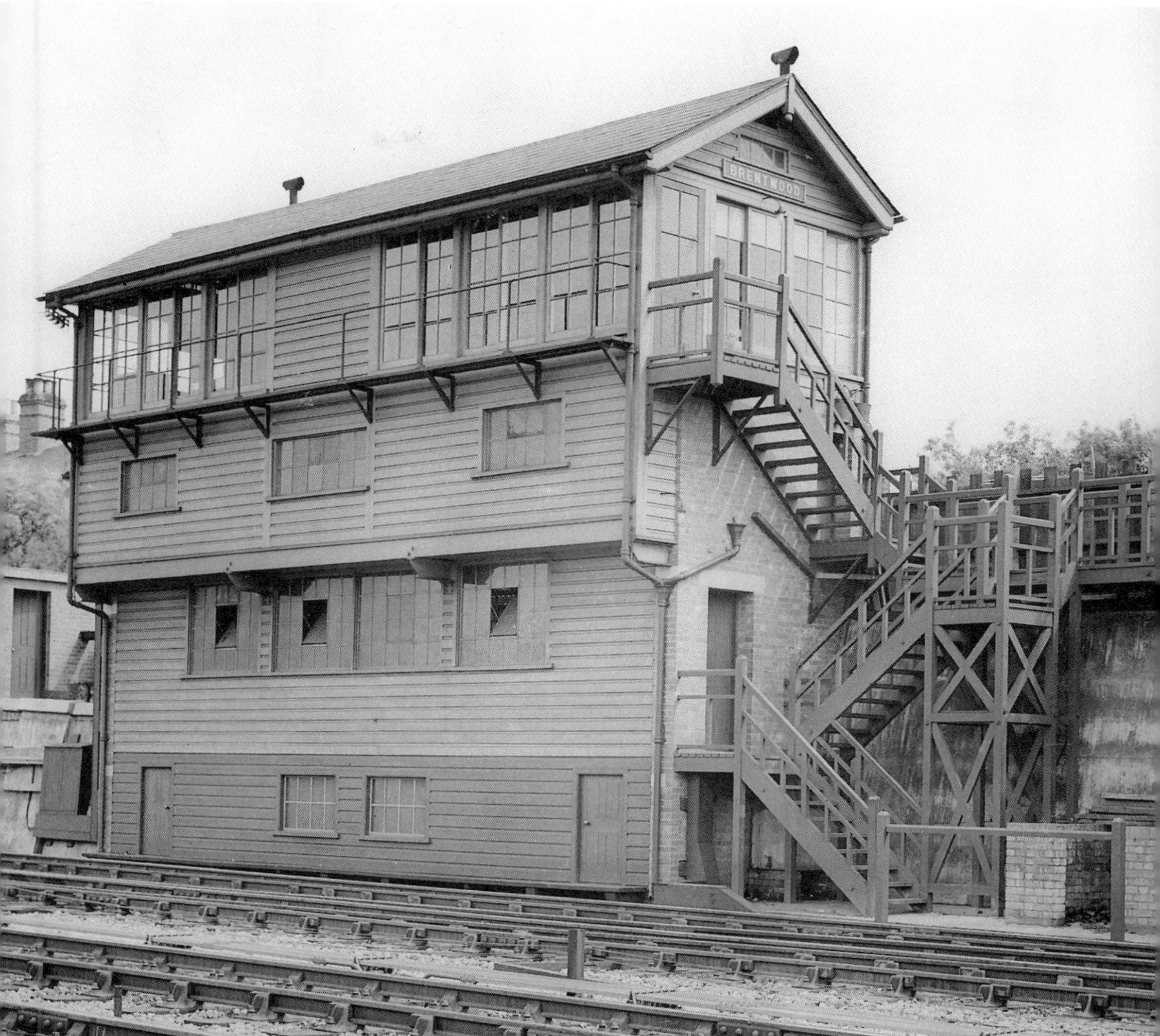
BRENTWOOD

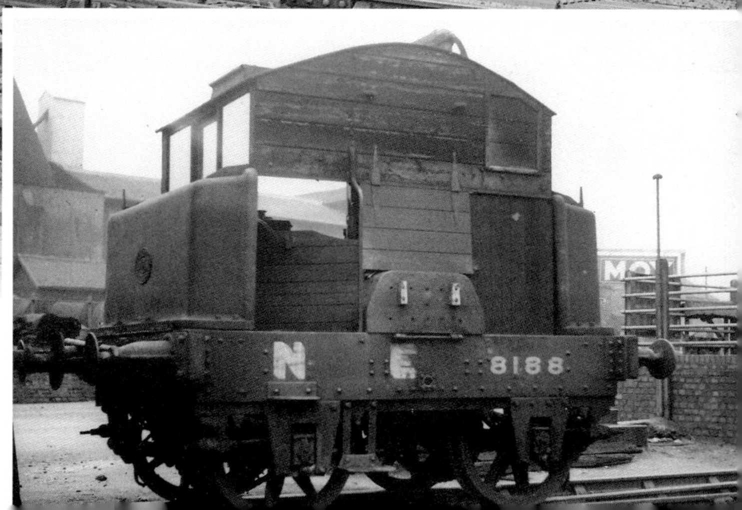
N E 8188

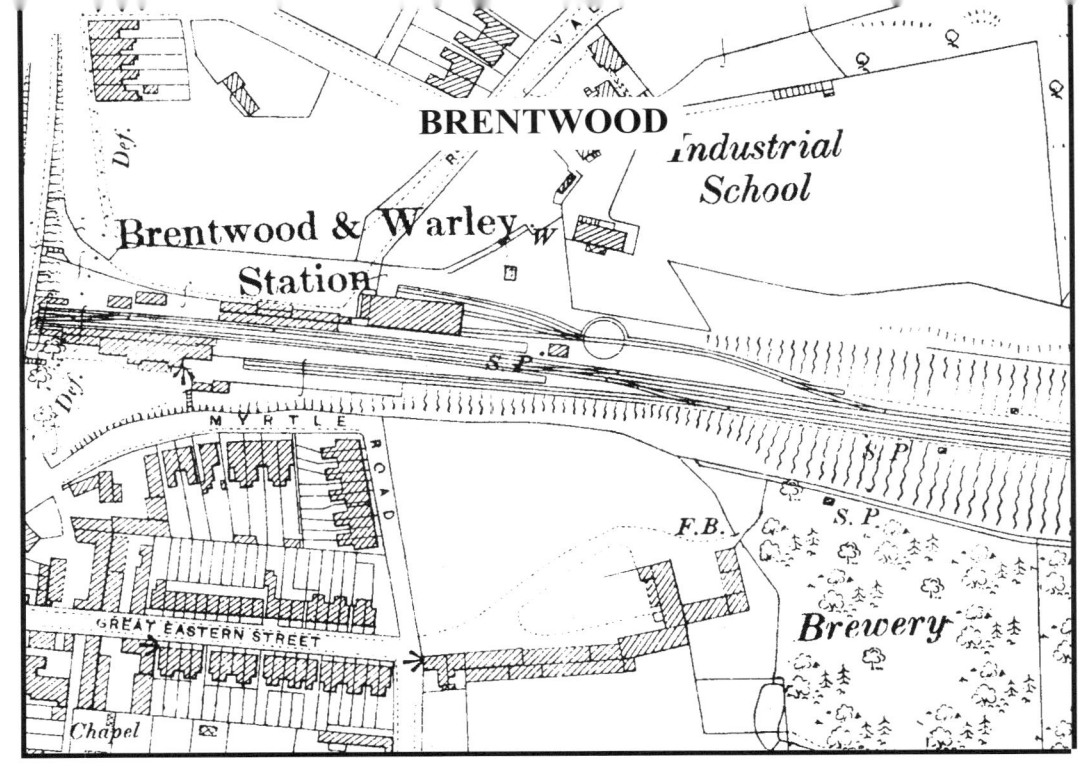

XIV. Brentwood opened on 1st July 1840. It became known as Brentwood & Warley on 1st November 1882 to reflect the growing catchment area. The GER reconstructed part of the station in 1904 and the LNER enlarged the station to four platforms, opening it on 1st January 1934. Although the suffix '& Warley' was dropped in 1969, the legend remained on the station nameboards for several years. Our OS extract from 1896 clearly shows the two-platform arrangement with the loco shed and turntable to the north of the line.

86. This evocative view provides a perfect illustration of the immense variety of freight traffic carried in pre-grouping days. Elaborately lettered furniture vans form part of a Parkeston bound freight as it leaves Brentwood yard on 29th April 1911. The locomotive is GER class T19 2-4-0 no. 743. (K.Nunn/LCGB)

87.	We are looking west on a very wet 23rd March 1912 as GER class S69 (LNER B12) storms up the incline with a Liverpool Street to Ipswich train. The distinctive tower on the platform building was demolished during the 1930s widening and to the right can be seen the engine shed. (K.Nunn/LCGB)

88.	One of the diminutive GER class C53 0-6-0 tram locomotives, no. 135, is seen here on the Brentwood turntable on 29th August 1912. The retaining wall still survives on this site and clearly indicates where the turntable once stood. (K.Nunn/LCGB)

89. This panorama is of the locomotive facilities looking east up the steepest part of the incline. The 3-road engine shed opened in 1872. Here we see the boiler house, turntable and coaling stage in this image from about 1915. (British Rail)

90. Taken from the cab of GER class S46 (LNER D14) 4-4-0 no. 1872 standing in the up loop, we have a good overall view of the station and engine shed during 1911. In the platform stands GER class T26 (LNER E4) 2-4-0 no. 1872, about to depart on a Liverpool Street to Southend Victoria service. (K.Nunn/LCGB)

91. The LNER 1930s widening gave rise to new station buildings, seen here devoid of any window frames in 1933. The stark contrast between the old order of the soon-to-be demolished GER signal box and the 'modern' ticket office provides us with a truly classic picture. (R.R.Clow/Harwich Shipping & Railway Museum)

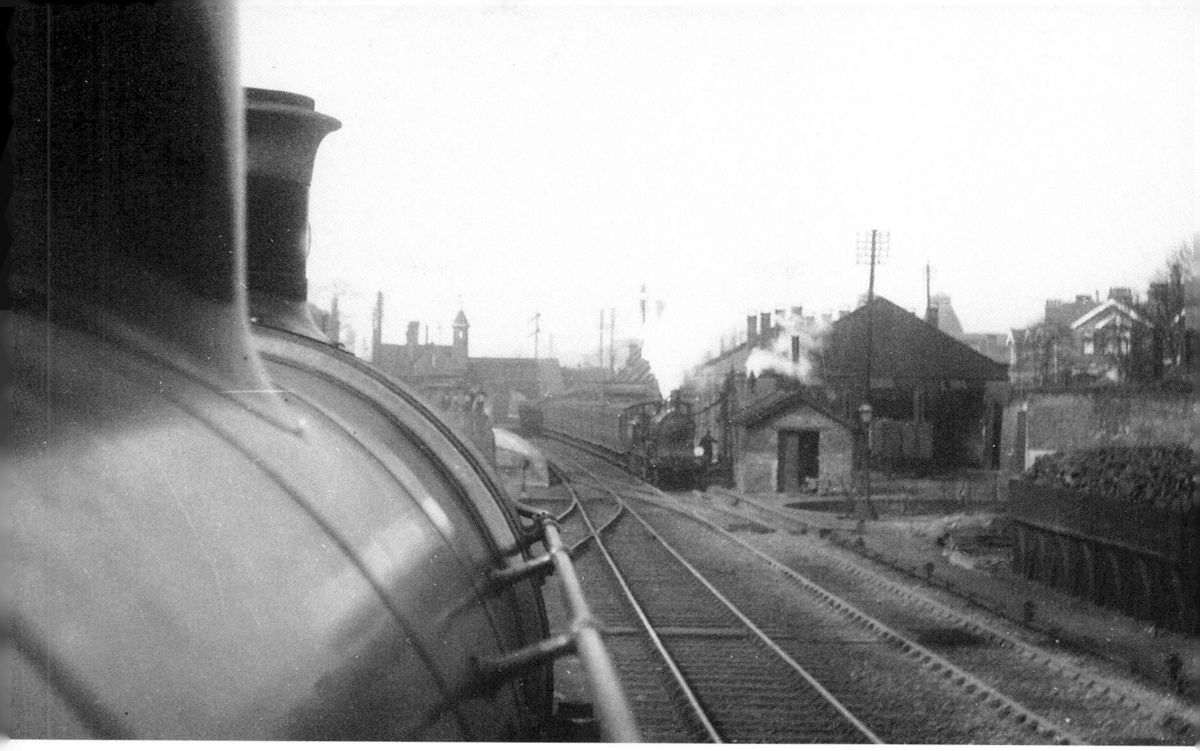

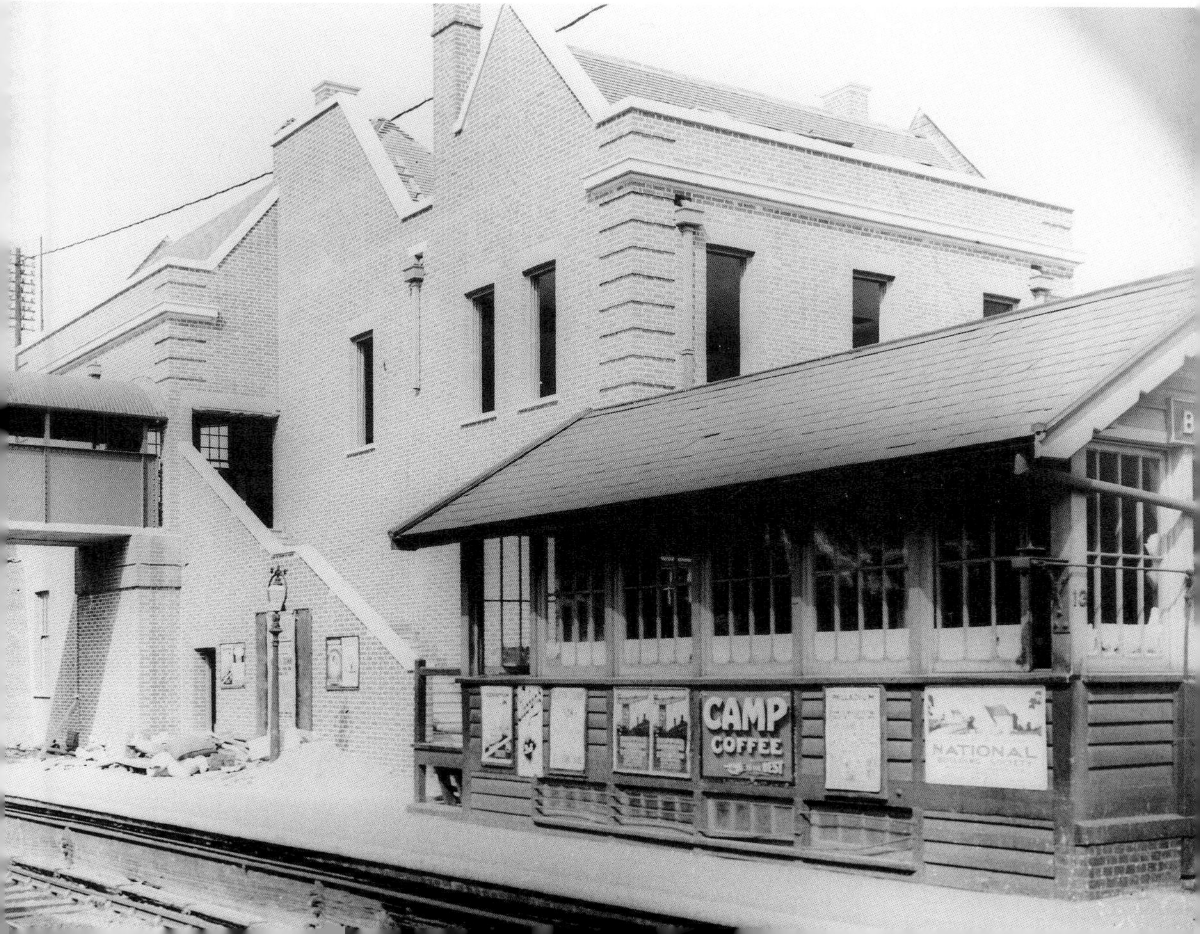
CAMP
COFFEE
NATIONAL

92. Here we see the widening work underway just east of the coal stage, as a new retaining wall is being constructed on the north side of the formation. The view is dated 12th October 1932. (British Rail)

93. This shows the attractive new station entrance buildings after the widening. The architectural style was described as 'chapelesque', although the only prayers said here were for the train to arrive on time. (Commercial postcard)

94. The terrible effects of the Second World War are illustrated after the 'Luftwaffe' had delivered its deadly cargo on 4th October 1940. At least one house has been totally flattened and both the train on the right, along with the platform, has sustained damage. Several locos stand outside the shed. (British Rail)

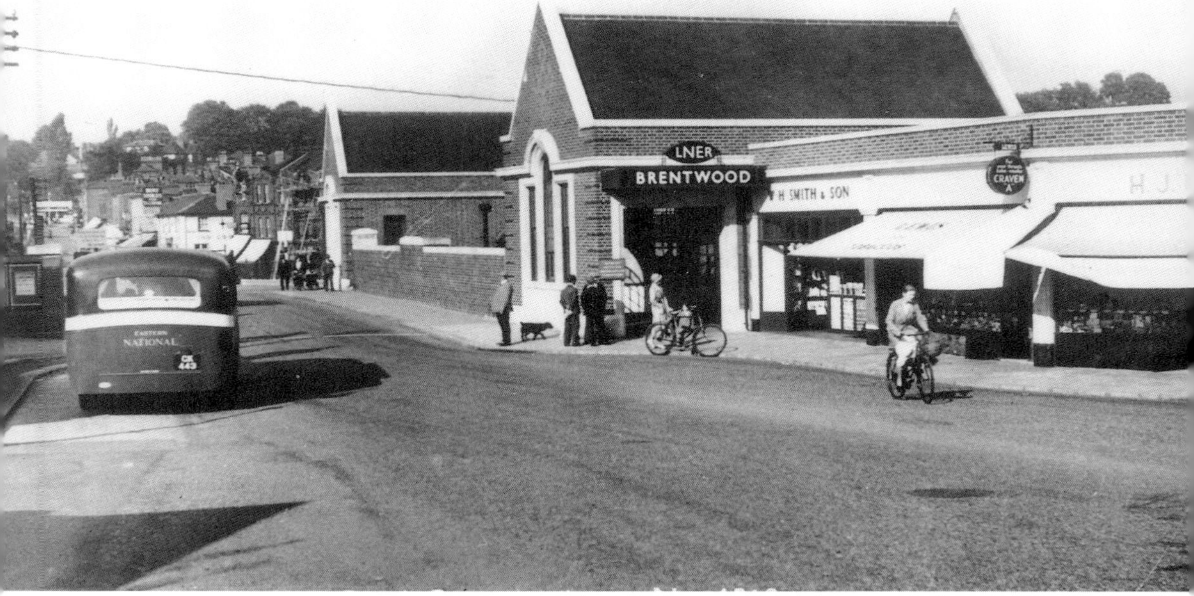
LNER
BRENTWOOD
W H SMITH & SON
CRAVEN A
EASTERN
NATIONAL

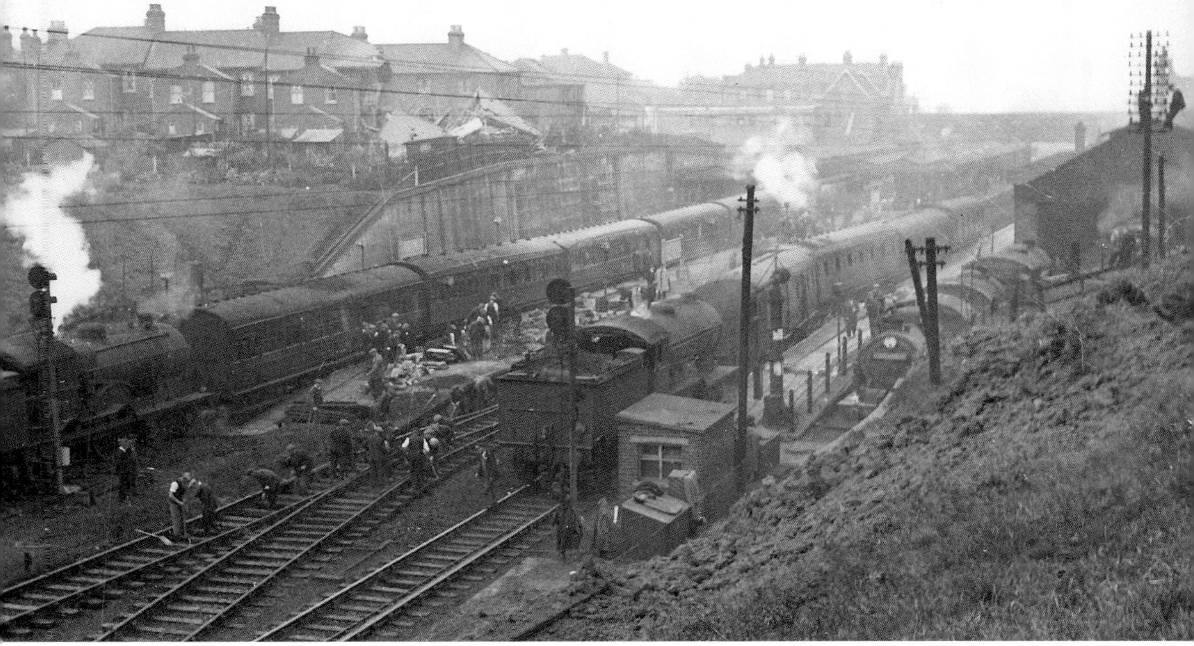

95. Although Brentwood shed closed in 1949, the site remained in this derelict state for many years. Our view looking west is dated 23rd July 1954. Amazingly, the spandrels supporting the platform awning on the Down Electric line have retained the Eastern Counties Railway initials in the ironwork to this day. (B.Pask)

96. Introduced in 1962, the class AM9 (later 309) Clacton and Walton EMUs brought huge benefits for passengers. Capable of 100 mph running, they gave sterling service until their withdrawal from GE metals on 3rd January 1994. Part of the fleet found its way to Manchester, but all were withdrawn by 2000. Here we see a Liverpool Street to Clacton service heading east on 30th April 1978. (A.Young)

97. We now witness a pair of class 86 locomotives, with No. 86631 leading, on a Freightliner as they descend the incline with a westbound service on 15th July 2002. Built as class AL6 in 1965 for West Coast Main Line express passenger work, these locomotives have proved themselves more than capable on heavy freight. (D.Brennand)

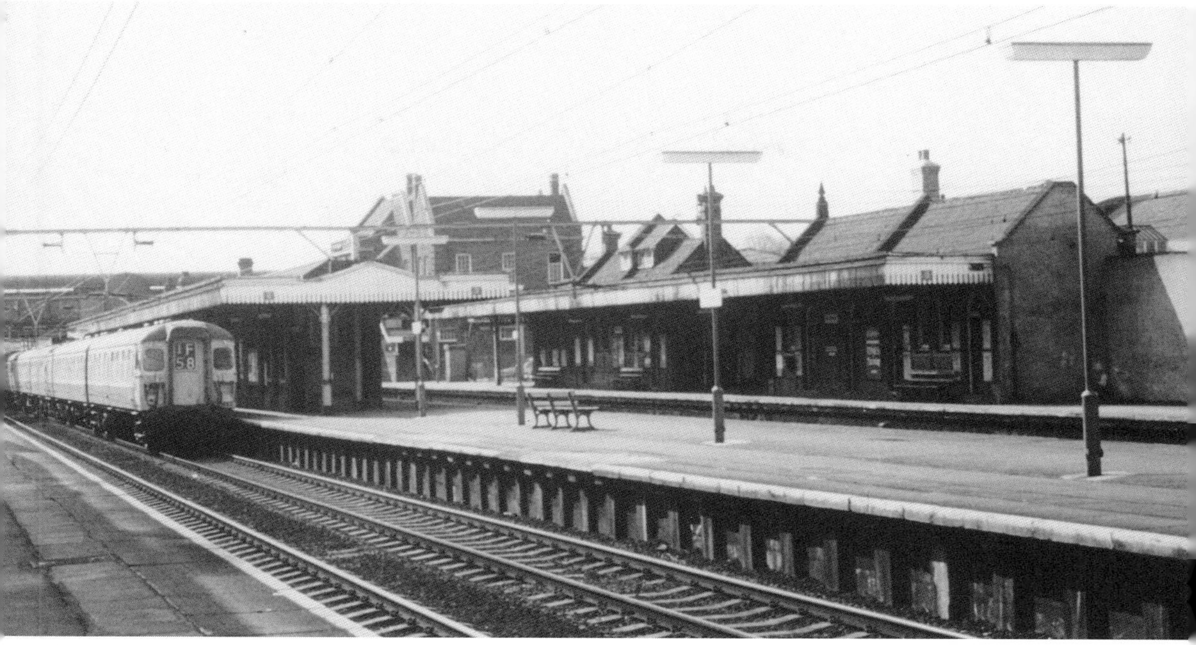

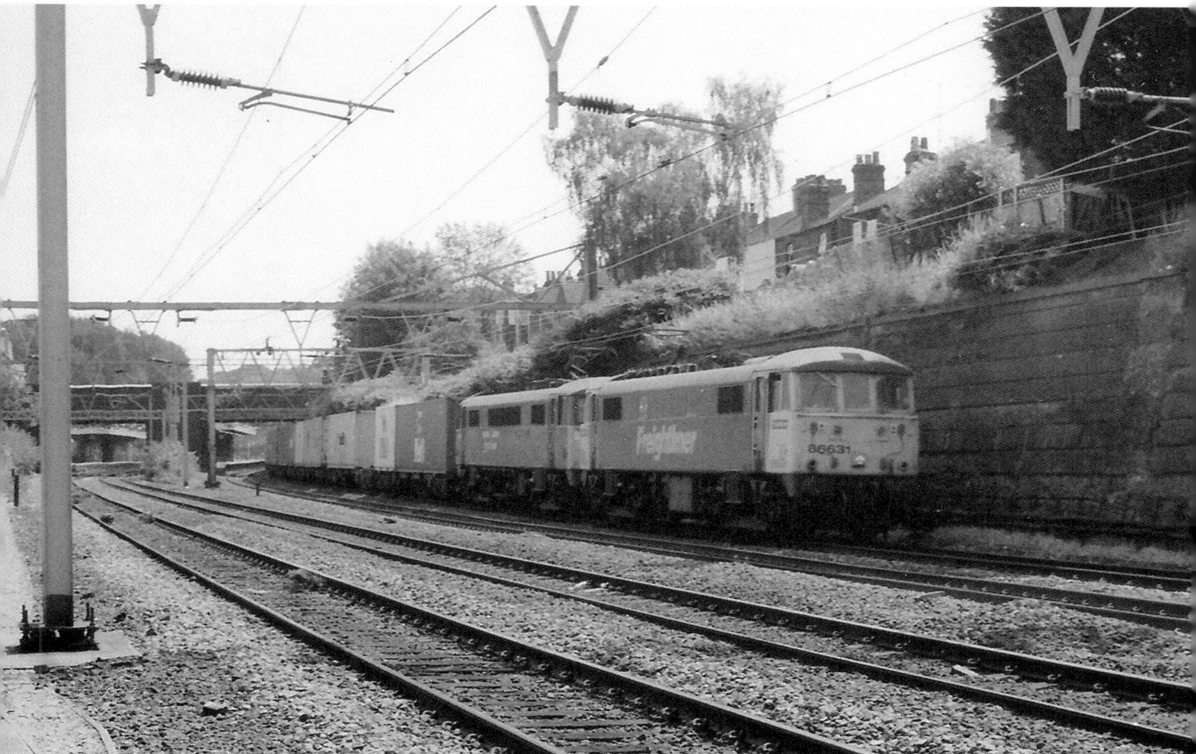
Freightliner
86631

EAST OF BRENTWOOD

98. This is Ingrave signal box at the top of Brentwood incline in 1911. The 1930s widening made the signal box redundant and it finally closed on 10th December 1933. (K.Nunn/LCGB)

99. One can almost sense the supreme effort of GER class C53 Tram Engine no. 127 as it struggles up the incline in full flight on its way from Stratford Works to Ipswich on 28th June 1914. Despite the huge cloud coming from the exhaust, the speed probably did not match the fireworks display. (K.Nunn/LCGB)

100. Here we can enjoy one of the most prestigious trains ever to have run over GE metals. LNER class D16/2 4-4-0 no. 8787 heads a Clacton to Liverpool Street service comprised entirely of Pullman stock as it descends the incline under the impressive Seven Arches Bridge on 15th June 1930. (K.Nunn/LCGB)

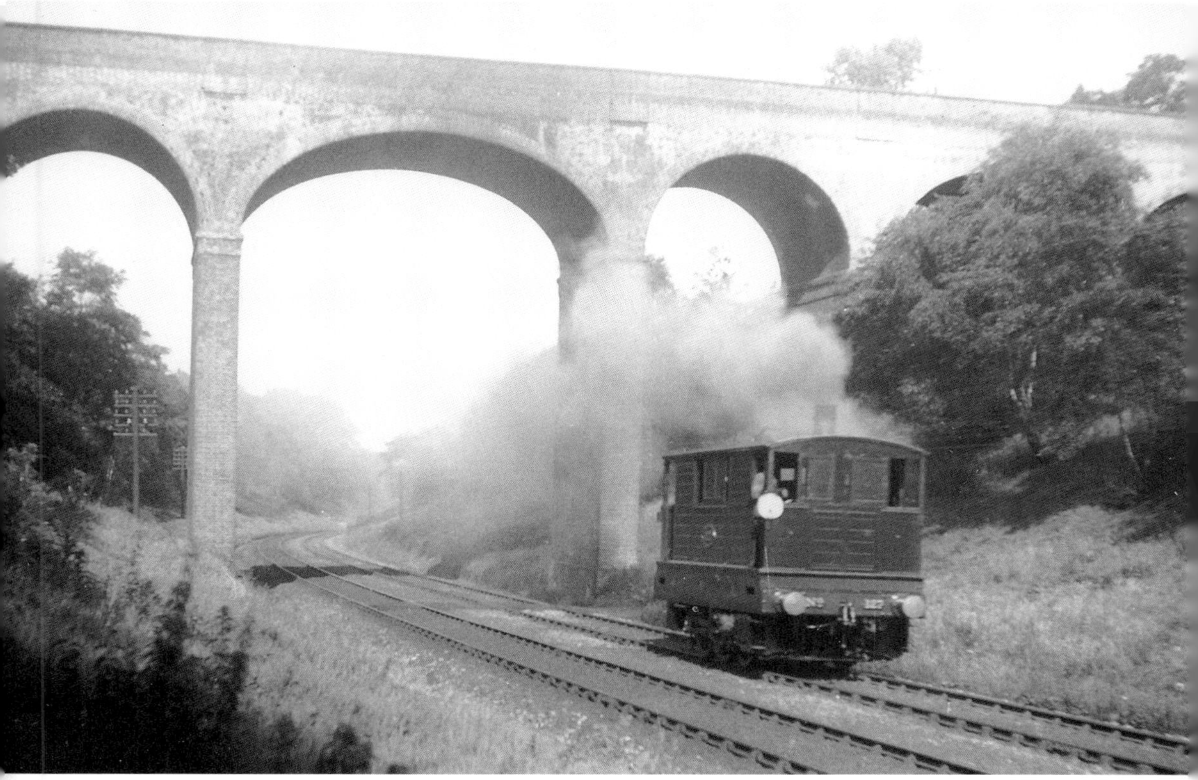

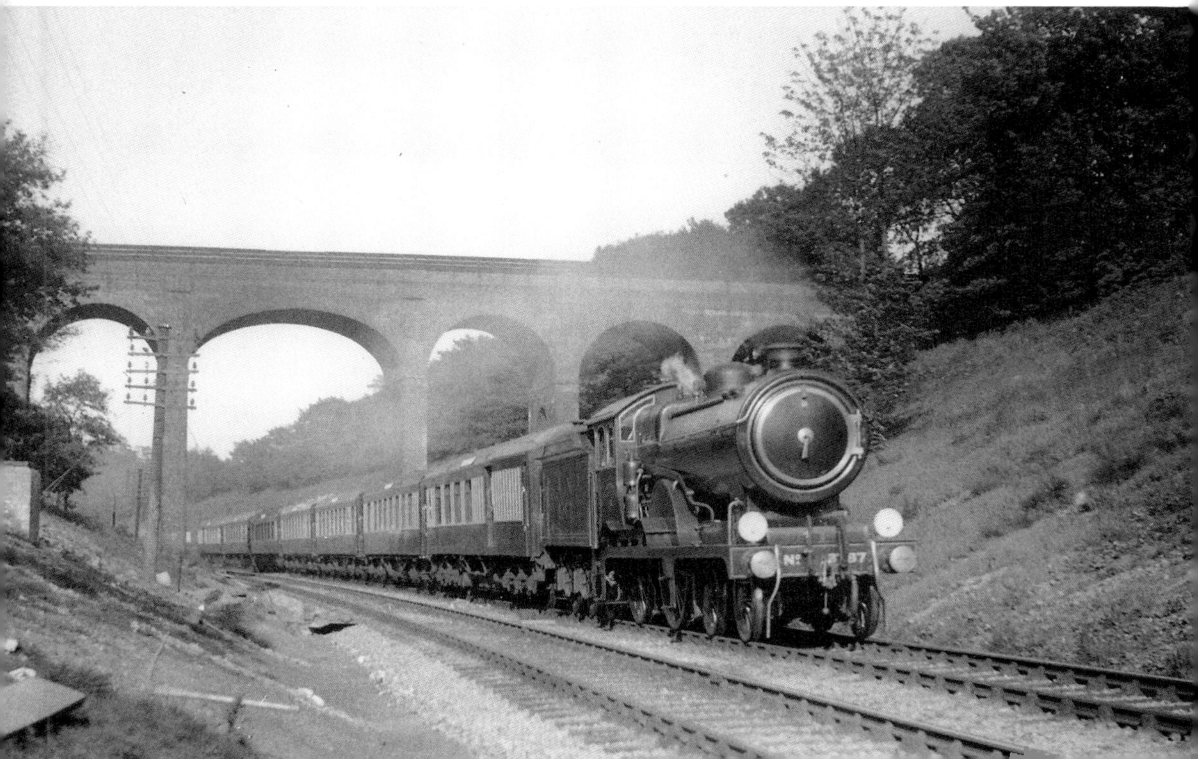

101. Approaching the summit is the short-lived streamlined LNER class B17/5 4-6-0 no. 2870 *City of London* with a Liverpool Street to Cromer express comprised of Gresley teak coaches. Being overtaken on the slow line is class B12 4-6-0 No. 8540 on a Liverpool Street to Southend Victoria service on 15th July 1939. (H.C.Casserley)

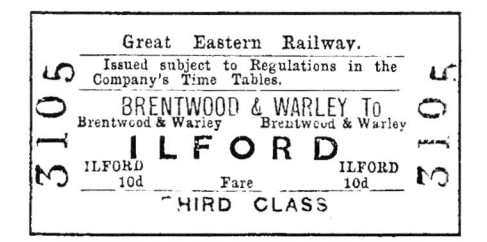

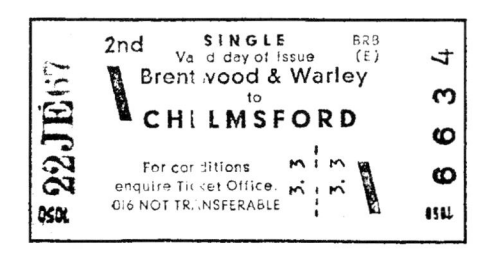

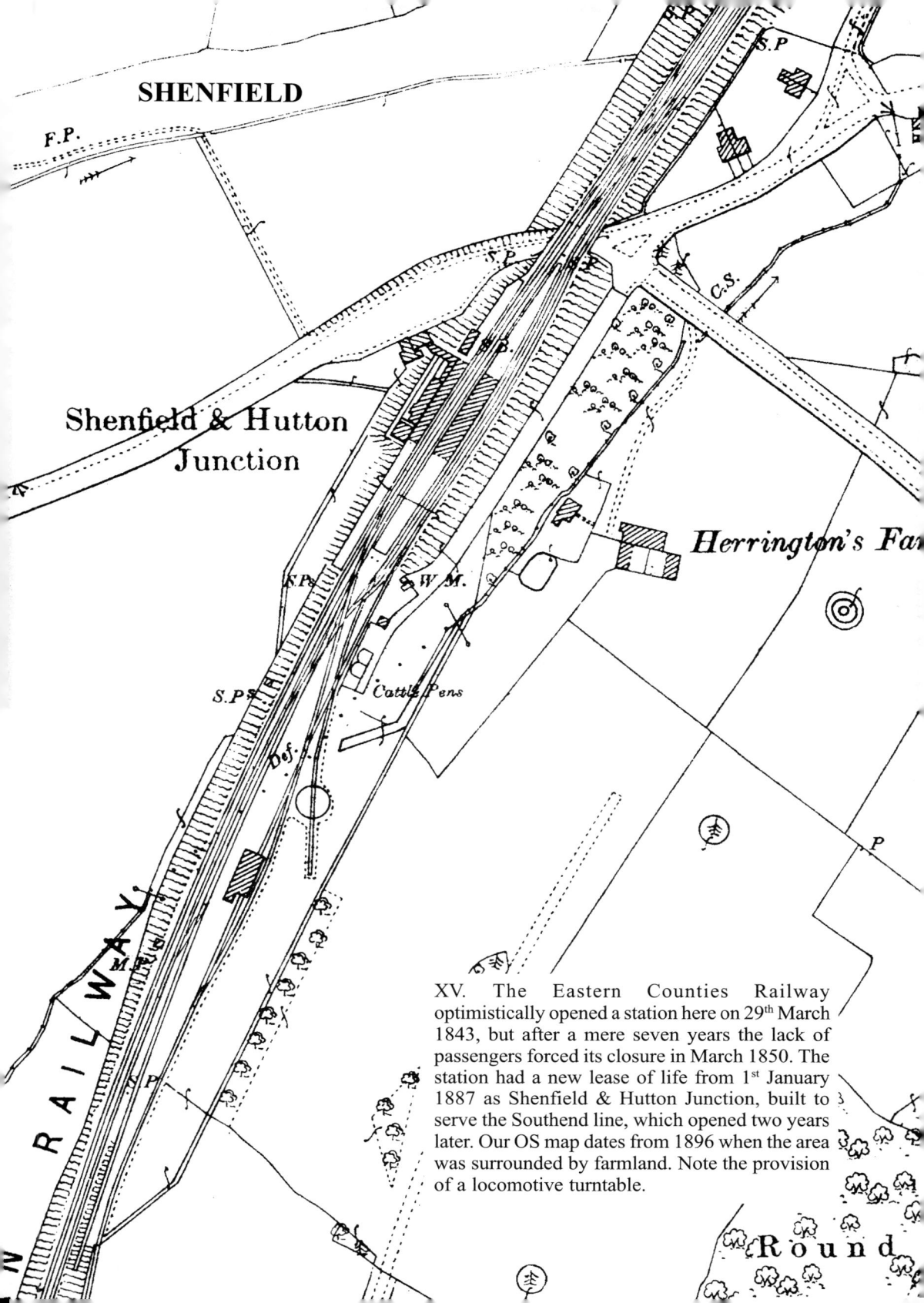

SHENFIELD

Shenfield & Hutton Junction

XV. The Eastern Counties Railway optimistically opened a station here on 29th March 1843, but after a mere seven years the lack of passengers forced its closure in March 1850. The station had a new lease of life from 1st January 1887 as Shenfield & Hutton Junction, built to serve the Southend line, which opened two years later. Our OS map dates from 1896 when the area was surrounded by farmland. Note the provision of a locomotive turntable.

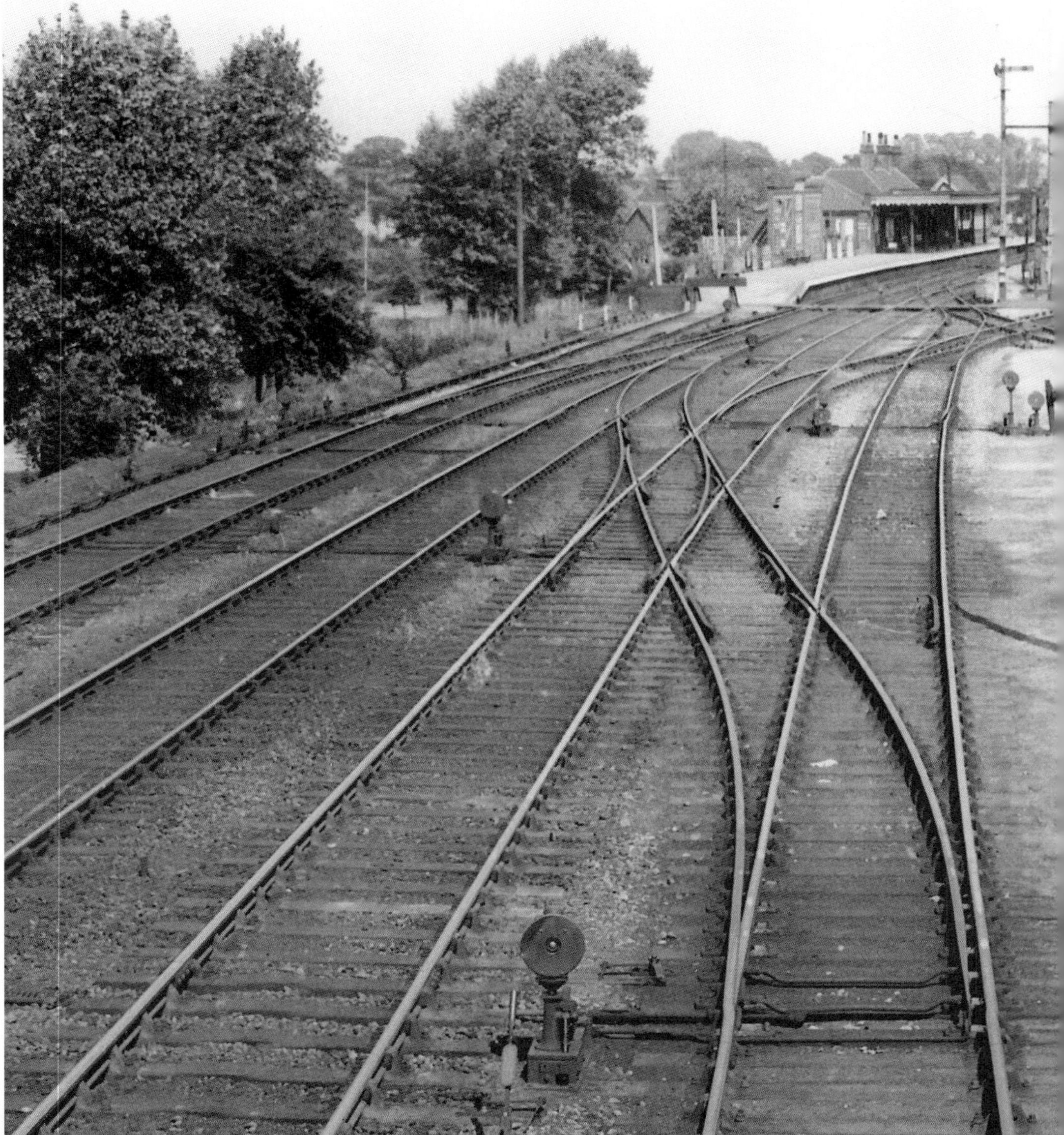

102. The station comprised of three platform faces, limited goods and loco facilities in this 1931 eastward view. A distinctive water tower and cattle dock subsequently gave way to the inevitable car park. Just out of view is the turntable.
(R.R.Clow/Harwich Shipping & Railway Museum)

103. Three years have lapsed since the previous view, and substantial investment has taken place to give two new platforms (4 and 5). We are looking west in January 1934 during reconstruction. A new signal box at the London end replaced the box on the platform shortly afterwards. (R.R.Clow/Harwich Shipping & Railway Museum)

104. Here we see the new signal box built during the widening programme. Note the absence of electrification masts in this view taken on 15th July 1939. The Second World War broke out just two months later. To the left can be seen the goods shed which was demolished in the 1960s to make way for the car park. (H.C.Casserley)

105. Despite the formation of British Railways on 1st January 1948, we see LNER classes B12 4-6-0 no. 1561 and B1 4-6-0 no. 1271 still clearly in LNER livery on 26th June in the same year. The pair are in charge of a Liverpool Street to Norwich service running east under the new overhead wires. (H.C.Casserley)

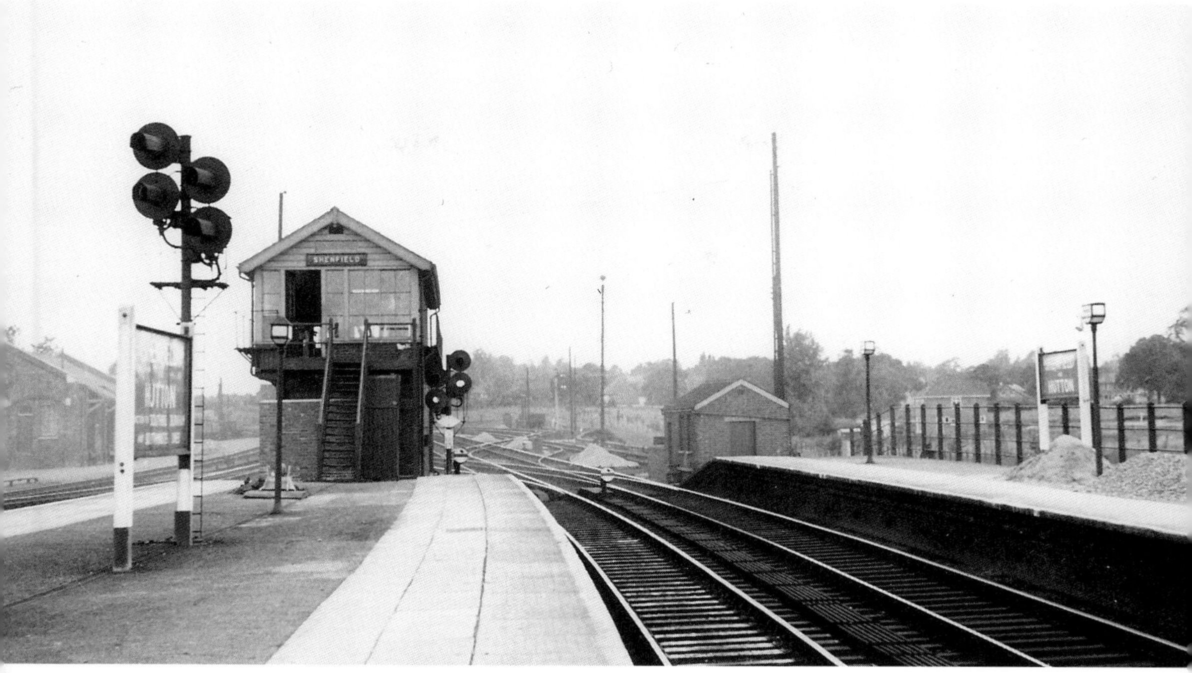
SHENFIELD

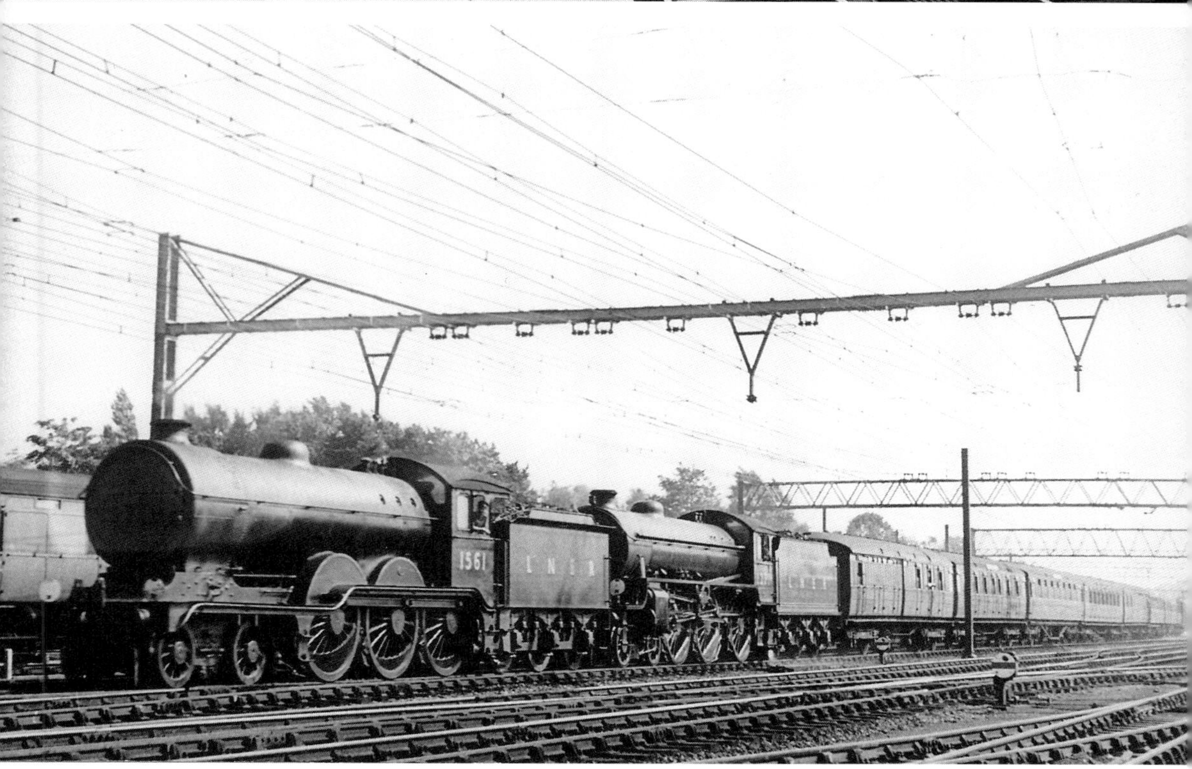
1561
L N E R

106. Just west of Shenfield we see a class 306 9-car train heading towards Liverpool Street and about to be overtaken by a steam hauled express on the main line. The view was taken on 8th October 1949. (K.Nunn/LCGB)

107. A glorious sunny day at Shenfield has tempted the day-trippers out. The EMU has disgorged its passengers, who are about to board a train to Southend hauled by class B1 4-6-0 no. 61363 on 1st September 1955. (T.Wright)

108. Taking day-trippers home again is class B17 4-6-0 no. 61610 *Honingham Hall* departing with a Southend to Liverpool Street train on 23rd September 1956. (B.Pask)

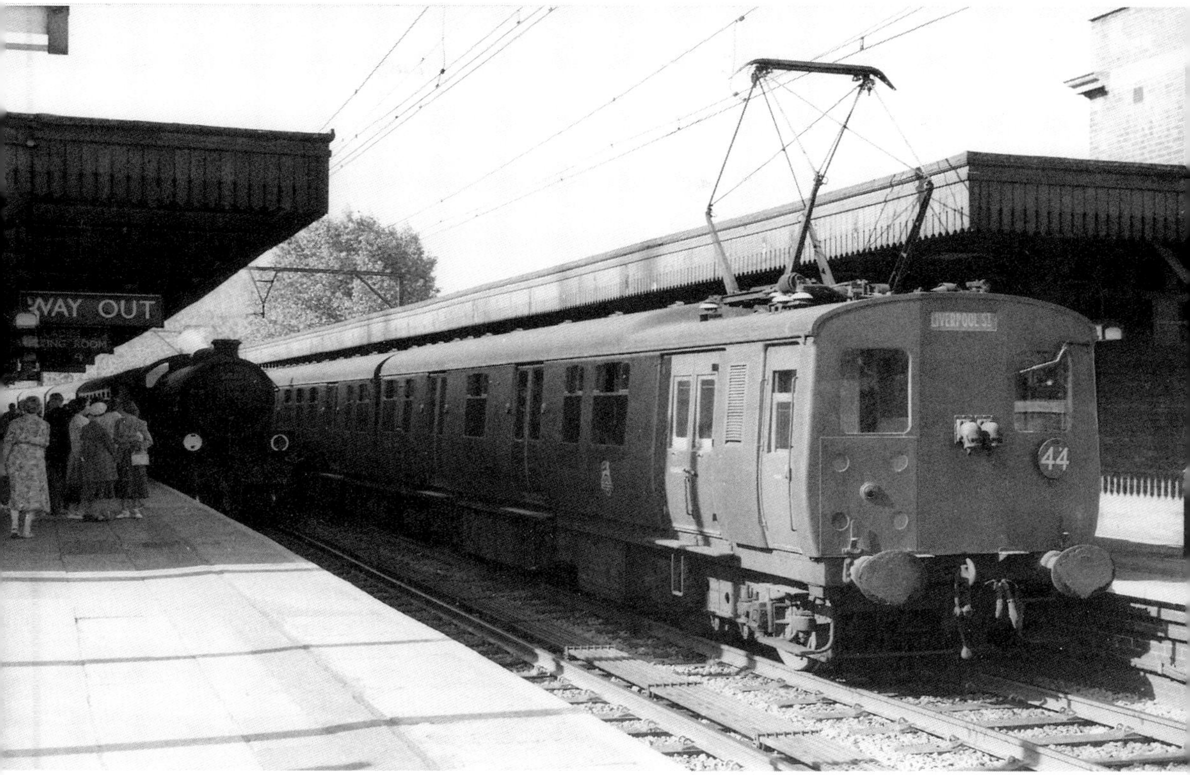
WAY OUT
LIVERPOOL ST.
44

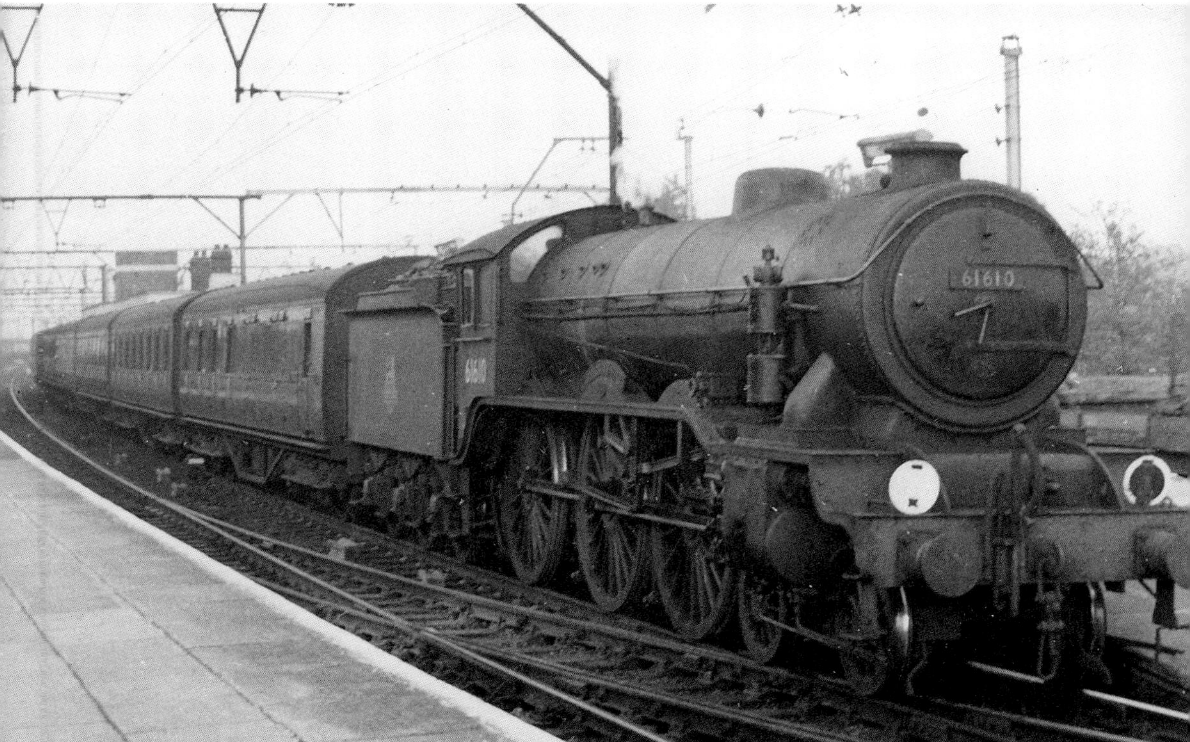
61610

109. Here we are treated to the rare sight of a weedkilling train taking on water in platform 1 on 24th September 1956. The locomotive is J15 0-6-0 no. 65470. The fireman on top of the tender is seemingly oblivious to the overhead wires above him. (B.Pask)

110. Now we can enjoy the "Essex Coast Express" hauled by 'Clan' class 4-6-2 no. 72009 *Clan Stewart* on its way from Liverpool Street to Clacton in September 1958. This loco regularly worked this train during its short visit to the former Great Eastern lines. (B.Pask)

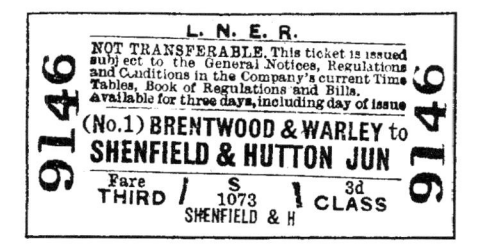

111. Working a breakdown train is a veteran class J15 0-6-0. It trundles through on its way from Stratford to deal with a mishap in the early months of 1958. The signal box closed in May 1981. (B.Pask)

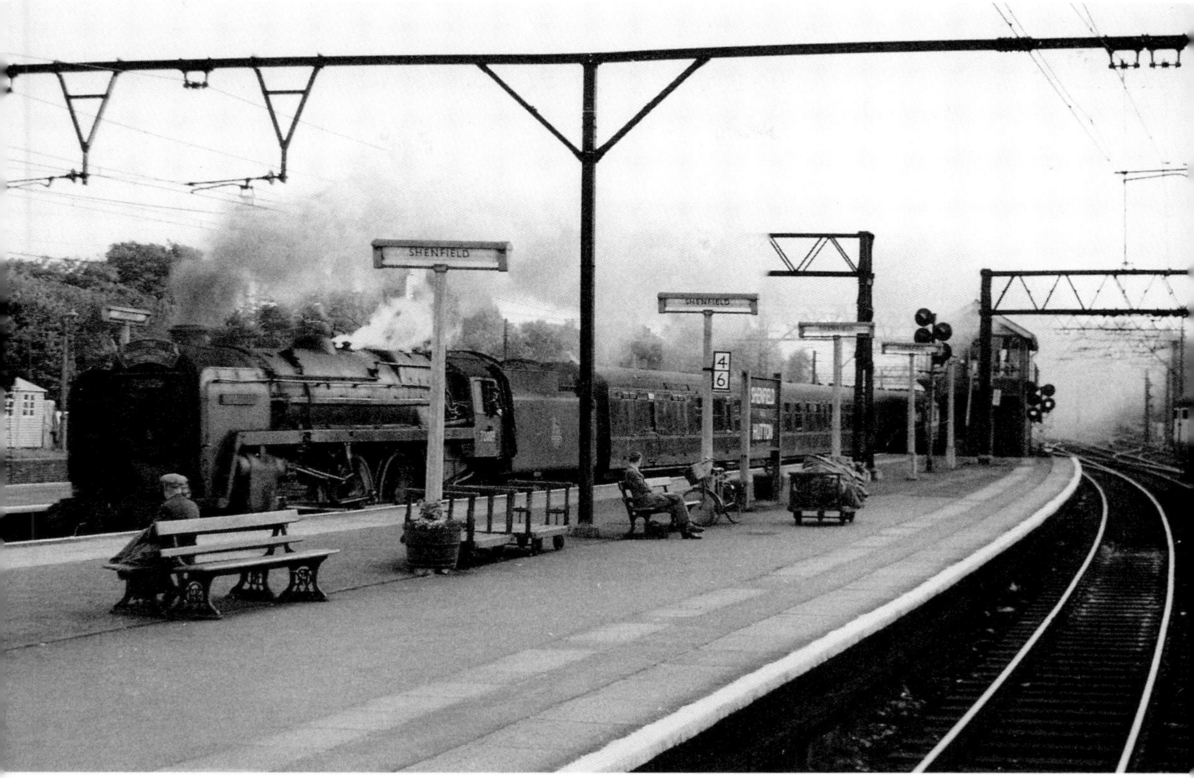
SHENFIELD
SHENFIELD
4
6

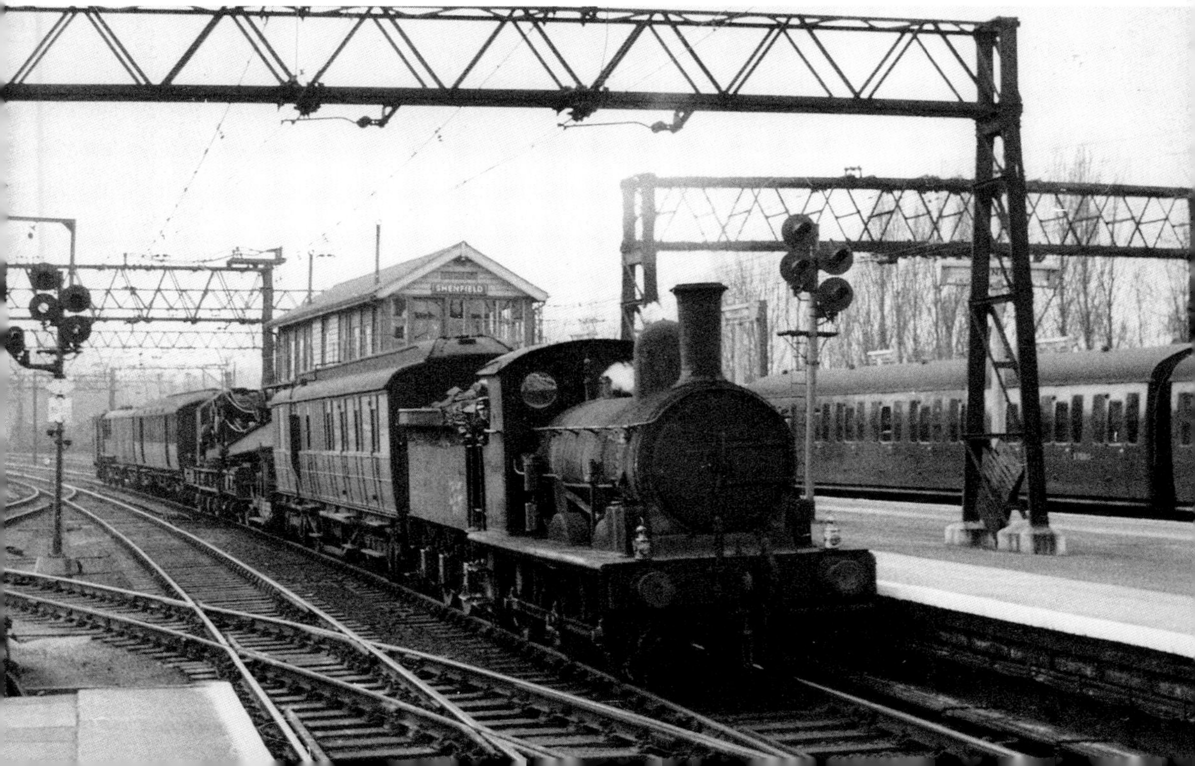
SHENFIELD

112. Upon their introduction in 1958, six of the first ten English Electric Type 4s to enter service found themselves elevated to Liverpool Street - Norwich workings. They did not perform any better than the "Britannia's" they replaced however. Here is no. D202 in 1958 as it leaves with a London bound express. (K.Nunn/LCGB)

113. Another of the 'pilot scheme' diesels to grace GE metals at a very early date were the "Toffee Apple" Brush Type 2s (class 31/0). Their nickname is derived from the drivers' control handle, which resembled a toffee apple. We see no. D5504 leaving with a London bound train on 14th June 1958. (A.R.Goult)

114. A Hymek diesel was a very rare sight on the route. No. D7053 was working a return excursion from Clacton to Reading in appalling holiday weather on 28th June 1964. (B.Pask)

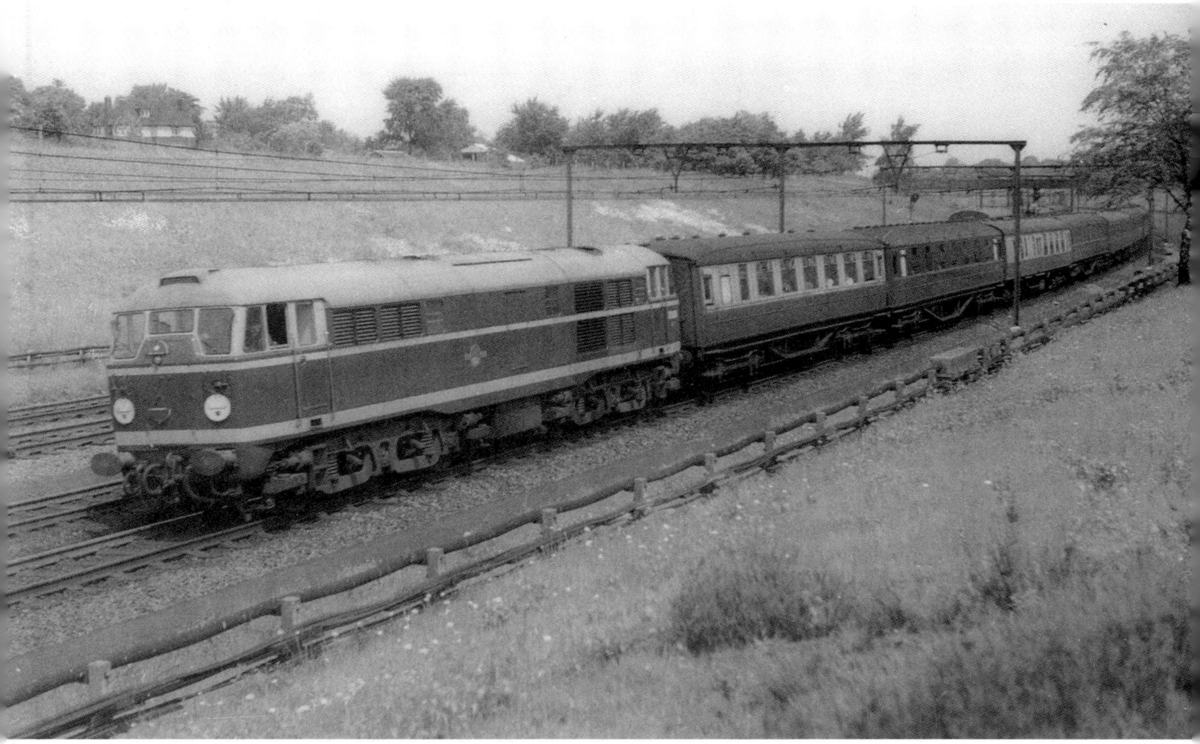

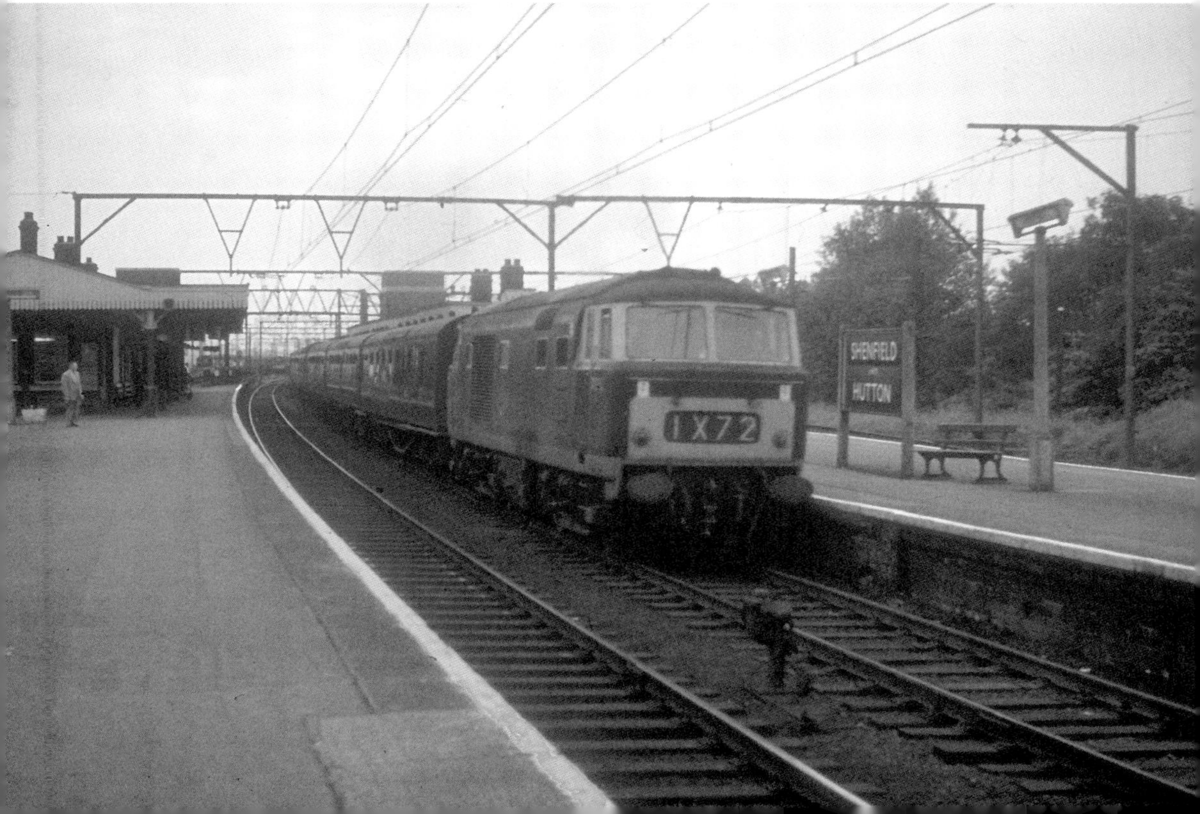

1X72
SHENFIELD
HUTTON

115. Standing on a Liverpool Street to Clacton train in the early 1960s is Brush Type 2 no. D5510. We are looking west. (K.Nunn/LCGB)

116. Here we see class 86 no. 86221 passing through the station with a Norwich to Liverpool Street express on 15th July 2002. These locomotives work on the push-pull system, with a DBSO coach at the country end. (D.Brennand)

117. The newest stock arrival has been Anglia Railways class 170 DMUs operating in 2 and 3-car sets. These stylish state-of-the-art machines have been popular with passengers and staff. Seen here on a Witham to Basingstoke service is no. 170399 on 8th July 2002. They were also employed on services to the East Suffolk line and to Norwich from London. The Basingstoke trains ceased to run in September 2002. (D.Brennand)

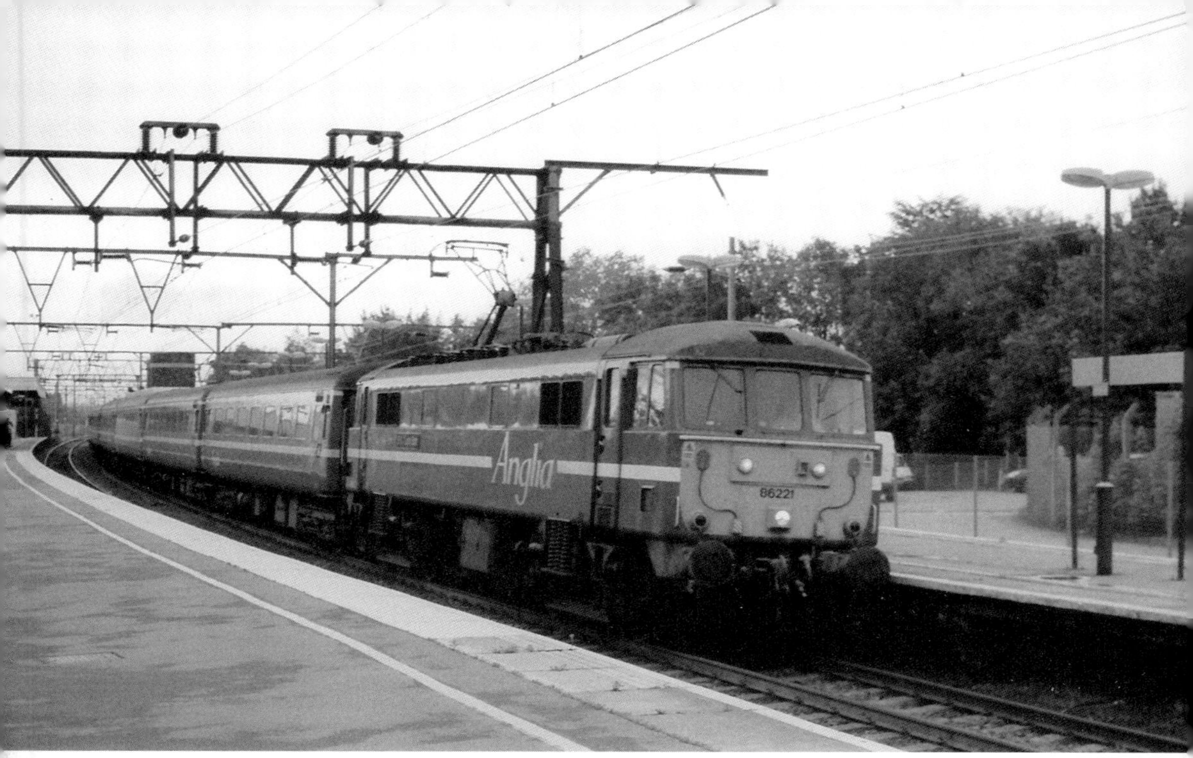
Anglia
86221

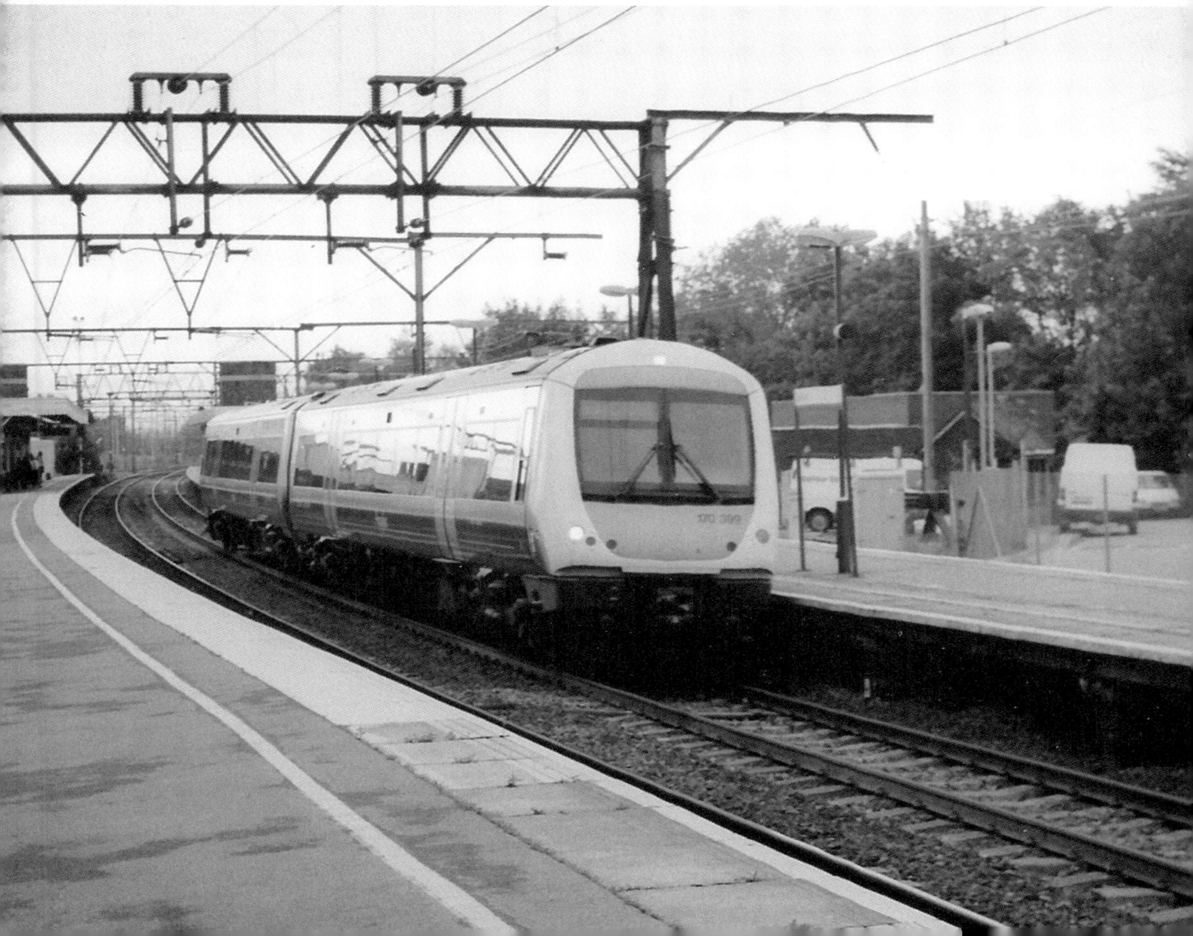
170 399

118. Powerful General Motor's class 66 locomotives now handle the majority of freight traffic. Being somewhat less charismatic than their predecessors, they have gained the unflattering nickname "Sheds" from enthusiasts. Seen here with a mere two wagons is no. 66063 heading east on 15th July 2002. (D.Brennand)

119. Class 315 EMUs were introduced in 1978 to handle all the inner suburban workings. To the right is a class 321 EMU on a Clacton to Liverpool Street service on 15th July 2002. Many of the 1930s buildings have fortunately survived at platform level. (D.Brennand)

120. Shenfield's population rose from 1692 in 1901 to 5390 in 1961. The exterior was photographed in August 2002. The station frontage had been rebuilt in the 1970s. (D.Brennand)

Shenfield
315 817
First
Great Eastern

Welcome to Shenfield
P690 MHJ

Middleton Press
EVOLVING THE ULTIMATE RAIL ENCYCLOPEDIA

Easebourne Lane, Midhurst, West Sussex.
GU29 9AZ   Tel:01730 813169
www.middletonpress.co.uk   email:info@middletonpress.co.uk
A-0 906520   B-1 873793   C-1 901706   D-1 904474

OOP Out of Print at time of printing - Please check current availability   **BROCHURE AVAILABLE SHOWING NEW TITLES**

A
Abergavenny to Merthyr C 91 5
Aldgate & Stepney Tramways B 70 7
Allhallows - Branch Line to A 62 2
Alton - Branch Lines to A 11 8
Andover to Southampton A 82 7
Ascot - Branch Lines around A 64 9
Ashburton - Branch Line to B 95 2
Ashford - Steam to Eurostar B 67 7
Ashford to Dover A 48 7
Austrian Narrow Gauge D 04 7
Avonmouth - BL around D 42 X

B
Banbury to Birmingham D 27 6
Barking to Southend C 80 X
Barnet & Finchley Tramways B 93 6
Barry - Branch Lines around D 50 0
Basingstoke to Salisbury A 89 4
Bath Green Park to Bristol C 36 2
Bath to Evercreech Junction A 60 6
Bath Tramways B 86 3
Battle over Portsmouth 1940 A 29 0
Battle over Sussex 1940 A 79 7
Bedford to Wellingborough D 31 4
Betwixt Petersfield & Midhurst A 94 0
Blitz over Sussex 1941-42 B 35 9
Bodmin - Branch Lines around B 83 9
Bognor at War 1939-45 B 59 6
Bombers over Sussex 1943-45 B 51 0
Bournemouth & Poole Trys B 47 2
Bournemouth to Evercreech Jn A 46 0
Bournemouth to Weymouth A 57 6
Bournemouth Trolleybuses C 10 9
Bradford Trolleybuses D 19 5
Brecon to Neath D 43 8
Brecon to Newport D 16 0
Brickmaking in Sussex B 19 7
Brightons Tramways B 02 2 OOP
Brighton to Eastbourne A 16 9
Brighton to Worthing A 03 7
Brighton Trolleybuses D 34 9
Bristols Tramways B 57 X
Bristol to Taunton D 03 9
Bromley South to Rochester B 23 5
Bromsgrove to Gloucester D 73 X
Brunel - A railtour of his achievements D 74 8
Bude - Branch Line to B 29 4
Burnham to Evercreech Jn A 68 1
Burton & Ashby Tramways C 51 6

C
Camberwell & West Norwood Tys B 22 7
Cambridge to Ely D 55 1
Canterbury - Branch Lines around B 58 8
Cardiff Trolleybuses D 64 0
Caterham & Tattenham Corner B 25 1
Changing Midhurst C 15 X
Chard and Yeovil - BLs around C 30 3
Charing Cross to Dartford A 75 4
Charing Cross to Orpington A 96 7
Cheddar - Branch Line to B 90 1
Cheltenham to Andover C 43 5
Chesterfield Tramways D 37 3
Chesterfield Trolleybuses D 51 9
Chichester to Portsmouth A 14 2
Clapham & Streatham Trys B 97 9 OOP
Clapham Junction - 50 yrs C 06 0 OOP
Clapham Junction to Beckenham Jn B 36 7
Clevedon & Portishead - BLs to D 18 7
Collectors Trains, Trolleys & Trams D 29 2
Colonel Stephens D62 4
Cornwall Narrow Gauge D 56 X
Crawley to Littlehampton A 34 7
Cromer - Branch Lines around C 26 5
Croydons Tramways B 42 1
Croydons Trolleybuses B 73 1 OOP
Croydon to East Grinstead B 48 9
Crystal Palace (HL) & Catford Loop A 87 8

D
Darlington Trolleybuses D 33 0
Dartford to Sittingbourne B 34 0
Derby Tramways D 17 9
Derby Trolleybuses C 72 9
Derwent Valley - Branch Line to the D 06 3
Didcot to Banbury D 02 0
Didcot to Swindon C 84 2
Didcot to Winchester C 13 3
Dorset & Somerset Narrow Gauge D 76 4
Douglas to Peel C 88 5
Douglas to Port Erin C 55 9
Douglas to Ramsey D 39 X
Dovers Tramways B 24 3
Dover to Ramsgate A 78 9

E
Ealing to Slough C 42 7
Eastbourne to Hastings A 27 4
East Cornwall Mineral Railways D 22 5
East Croydon to Three Bridges A 53 3
East Grinstead - Branch Lines to A 07 X
East Ham & West Ham Tramways B 52 9
East Kent Light Railway A 61 4 OOP
East London - Branch Lines of C 44 3
East London Line B 80 4
East Ridings Secret Resistance D 21 7
Edgware & Willesden Tramways C 18 4
Effingham Junction - BLs around A 74 6
Eltham & Woolwich Tramways B 74 X OOP
Ely to Kings Lynn C 53 2
Ely to Norwich C 90 7
Embankment & Waterloo Tramways B 41 3
Enfield & Wood Green Trys C 03 6 OOP
Enfield Town & Palace Gates - BL to D 32 2
Epsom to Horsham A 30 4
Euston to Harrow & Wealdstone C 89 3
Exeter & Taunton Tramways B 32 4
Exeter to Barnstaple B 15 4
Exeter to Newton Abbot C 49 4
Exeter to Tavistock B 69 3
Exmouth - Branch Lines to B 00 6

F
Fairford - Branch Line to A 52 5
Falmouth, Helston & St. Ives - BL to C 74 5
Fareham to Salisbury A 67 3
Faversham to Dover B 05 7
Felixstowe & Aldeburgh - BL to D 20 9
Fenchurch Street to Barking C 20 6
Festiniog - 50 yrs of enterprise C 83 4
Festinog in the Fifties B 68 5
Festinog in the Sixties B 91 X
Finsbury Park to Alexandra Palace C 02 8
Frome to Bristol B 77 4
Fulwell - Trams, Trolleys & Buses D 11 X

G
Gloucester to Bristol D 35 7
Gloucester to Cardiff D 66 7
Gosport & Horndean Trys B 92 8
Gosport - Branch Lines around A 36 3
Great Yarmouth Tramways D 13 6
Greece Narrow Gauge D 72 1
Greenwich & Dartford Tramways B 14 6 OOP
Guildford to Redhill A 63 0

H
Hammersmith & Hounslow Trys C 33 8
Hampshire Narrow Gauge D 36 5
Hampshire Waterways A 84 3 OOP
Hampstead & Highgate Tramways B 53 7
Harrow to Watford D 14 4
Hastings to Ashford A 37 1 OOP
Hastings Tramways B 18 9
Hastings Trolleybuses B 81 2 OOP
Hawkhurst - Branch Line to A 66 5
Hayling - Branch Line to A 12 6
Haywards Heath to Seaford A 28 2
Henley, Windsor & Marlow - BL to C77 X
Hereford to Newport D 54 3
Hexham to Carlisle D 75 6
Hitchin to Peterborough D 07 1
Holborn & Finsbury Tramways B 79 0
Holborn Viaduct to Lewisham A 81 9
Horsham - Branch Lines to A 02 9
Huddersfield Trolleybuses C 92 3
Hull Tramways D60 8
Hull Trolleybuses D 24 1
Huntingdon - Branch Lines around A 93 2

I
Ilford & Barking Tramways B 61 8
Ilford to Shenfield C 97 4
Ilfracombe - Branch Line to B 21 9
Ilkeston & Glossop Tramways D 40 3
Industrial Rlys of the South East A 09 6
Ipswich to Saxmundham C 41 9
Ipswich Trolleybuses D 59 4
Isle of Wight Lines - 50 yrs C 12 5

K
Kent & East Sussex Waterways A 72 X
Kent Narrow Gauge C 45 1
Kent Seaways - Hoys to Hovercraft D 79 9
Kingsbridge - Branch Line to C 98 2
Kingston & Hounslow Loops A 83 5 OOP
Kingston & Wimbledon Tramways B 56 1
Kingswear - Branch Line to C 17 6

L
Lambourn - Branch Line to C 70 2
Launceston & Princetown - BL to C 19 2
Lewisham & Catford Tramways B 26 X OOP

Lewisham to Dartford A 92 4
Lines around Wimbledon B 75 8
Liverpool Street to Chingford D 01 2
Liverpool Street to Ilford C 34 6
Liverpool Tramways - Eastern C 04 4
Liverpool Tramways - Northern C 46 X
Liverpool Tramways - Southern C 23 0
London Bridge to Addiscombe B 20 0
London Bridge to East Croydon A 58 4
London Chatham & Dover Railway A 88 6
London Termini - Past and Proposed D 00 4
London to Portsmouth Waterways B 43 X
Longmoor - Branch Lines to A 41 X
Looe - Branch Line to C 22 2
Lyme Regis - Branch Line to A 45 2
Lynton - Branch Line to B 04 9

M
Maidstone & Chatham Tramways B 40 5
Maidstone Trolleybuses C 00 1 OOP
March - Branch Lines around B 09 X
Margate & Ramsgate Tramways C 52 4
Marylebone to Rickmansworth D49 7
Midhurst - Branch Lines around A 49 5
Midhurst - Branch Lines to A 01 0 OOP
Military Defence of West Sussex A 23 1
Military Signals, South Coast C 54 0
Minehead - Branch Line to A 80 0
Mitcham Junction Lines B 01 4
Mitchell & company C 59 1
Monmouthshire Eastern Valleys D 71 3
Moreton-in-Marsh to Worcester D 26 8
Moretonhampstead - BL to C 27 3

N
Newbury to Westbury C 66 4
Newcastle to Hexham D 69 1
Newcastle Trolleybuses D 78 0
Newport (IOW) - Branch Lines to A 26 6
Newquay - Branch Lines to C 71 0
Newton Abbot to Plymouth C 60 5
Northern France Narrow Gauge C 75 3
North East German Narrow Gauge D 44 6
North Kent Tramways B 44 8
North London Line B 94 4
North Woolwich - BLs around C 65 6
Norwich Tramways C 40 0
Nottinghamshire & Derbyshire T/B D 63 2
Nottinghamshire & Derbyshire T/W D 53 5

O
Orpington to Tonbridge B 03 0 OOP
Oxford to Bletchley D57 8
Oxford to Moreton-in-Marsh D 15 2

P
Paddington to Ealing C 37 0
Paddington to Princes Risborough C 81 8
Padstow - Branch Line to B 54 5
Plymouth - BLs around B 98 7
Plymouth to St. Austell C 63 X
Pontypool to Mountain Ash D 65 9
Porthmadog 1954-94 - BL around B 31 6
Porthmadog to Blaenau B 50 2 OOP
Portmadoc 1923-46 - BL around B 13 8
Portsmouths Tramways B 72 3
Portsmouth to Southampton A 31 2
Portsmouth Trolleybuses C 73 7
Potters Bar to Cambridge D 70 5
Princes Risborough - Branch Lines to D 05 5
Princes Risborough to Banbury C 85 0

R
Railways to Victory C 16 8/7 OOP
Reading to Basingstoke B 27 8
Reading to Didcot C 79 6
Reading to Guildford A 47 9 OOP
Reading Tramways B 87 1
Reading Trolleybuses C 05 2
Redhill to Ashford A 73 8
Return to Blaenau 1970-82 C 64 8
Rickmansworth to Aylesbury D 61 6
Roman Roads of Hampshire D 67 5
Roman Roads of Surrey C 61 3
Roman Roads of Sussex C 48 6
Romneyrail C 32 X
Ryde to Ventnor A 19 3

S
Salisbury to Westbury B 39 1
Salisbury to Yeovil B 06 5 OOP
Saxmundham to Yarmouth C 69 9
Saxony Narrow Gauge D 47 0
Seaton & Eastbourne Tramways B 76 6 OOP
Seaton & Sidmouth - Branch Lines A 95 9
Secret Sussex Resistance B 82 0
SECR Centenary album C 11 7
Selsey - Branch Line to A 04 5

Sheerness - Branch Lines around B 16 2
Shepherds Bush to Uxbridge T/Ws C 28 1
Shrewsbury - Branch Line to A 86 X
Sierra Leone Narrow Gauge D 28 4
Sittingbourne to Ramsgate A 90 8
Slough to Newbury C 56 7
Solent - Creeks, Crafts & Cargoes D 52 7
Southamptons Tramways B 33 2
Southampton to Bournemouth A 42 8
Southend-on-Sea Tramways B 28 6
Southern France Narrow Gauge C 47 8
Southwark & Deptford Tramways B 38 3
Southwold - Branch Line to A 15 0
South Eastern & Chatham Railways C 08
South London Line B 46 4
South London Tramways 1903-33 D 10 1
St. Albans to Bedford D 08 X
St. Austell to Penzance C 67 2
St. Pancras to Barking D 68 3
St. Pancras to St. Albans C 78 8
Stamford Hill Tramways B 85 5
Steaming through Cornwall B 30 8 OOP
Steaming through Kent A 13 4 OOP
Steaming through the Isle of Wight A 56 8
Steaming through West Hants A 69 X
Stratford upon avon to Birmingham D 772
Stratford upon Avon to Cheltenham C 25 7
Strood to Paddock Wood B 12 X
Surrey Home Guard C 57 5
Surrey Narrow Gauge C 87 7
Surrey Waterways A 51 7 OOP
Sussex Home Guard C 24 9
Sussex Narrow Gauge C 68 0
Sussex Shipping Sail, Steam & Motor D 23
Swanley to Ashford B 45 6
Swindon to Bristol C 96 6
Swindon to Gloucester D46 2
Swindon to Newport D 30 6
Swiss Narrow Gauge C 94 X

T
Talyllyn - 50 years C 39 7
Taunton to Barnstaple B 60 X
Taunton to Exeter C 82 6
Tavistock to Plymouth B 88 X
Tees-side Trolleybuses D 58 6
Tenterden - Branch Line to A 21 5
Thanet's Tramways B 11 1 OOP
Three Bridges to Brighton A 35 5
Tilbury Loop C 86 9
Tiverton - Branch Lines around C 62 1
Tivetshall to Beccles D 41 1
Tonbridge to Hastings A 44 4
Torrington - Branch Lines to B 37 5
Tunbridge Wells - Branch Lines to A 32 0
Twickenham & Kingston Trys C 35 4
Two-Foot Gauge Survivors C 21 4 OOP

U
Upwell - Branch Line to B 64 2

V
Victoria & Lambeth Tramways B 49 9
Victoria to Bromley South A 98 3
Victoria to East Croydon A 40 1 OOP
Vivarais C 31 1

W
Walthamstow & Leyton Tramways B 65 0
Waltham Cross & Edmonton Trys C 07 9
Wandsworth & Battersea Tramways B 63
Wantage - Branch Line to D 25 X
Wareham to Swanage - 50 yrs D 09 8
War on the Line A 10 X
War on the Line VIDEO + 88 0
Waterloo to Windsor A 54 1
Waterloo to Woking A 38 X
Watford to Leighton Buzzard D 45 4
Wenford Bridge to Fowey C 09 5
Westbury to Bath B 55 3
Westbury to Taunton C 76 1
West Cornwall Mineral Railways D 48 9
West Croydon to Epsom B 08 1
West London - Branch Lines of C 50 8
West London Line B 84 7
West Sussex Waterways A 24 X OOP
West Wiltshire - Branch Lines of D 12 8
Weymouth - Branch Lines around A 65 7
Willesden Junction to Richmond B 71 5
Wimbledon to Beckenham C 58 3
Wimbledon to Epsom B 62 6
Wimborne - Branch Lines around A 97 5
Wisbech - Branch Lines around C 01 X
Wisbech 1800-1901 C 93 1
Woking to Alton A 59 2
Woking to Portsmouth A 25 8
Woking to Southampton A 55 X
Woolwich & Dartford Trolleys B 66 9 OOP
Worcester to Hereford D 38 1
Worthing to Chichester A 06 1

Y
Yeovil - 50 yrs change C 38 9
Yeovil to Dorchester A 76 2 OOP
Yeovil to Exeter A 91 6

96